KURT COBAIN & **COURTNEY LOVE** *In Their Own Words*

Nick Wise

D1450838

Kurt &
Courtney
"Talking"

OMNIBUS PRESS

KURT & **COURTNEY** *Talking*

Cover & Book designed by Fresh Lemon.
Picture research by Nikki Russell & Sarah Bacon.

ISBN: 1.84449.098.X
Order No: OP49885

Exclusive Distributors:
Music Sales Limited,
8/9 Frith Street, London W1D 3JB, UK.

Music Sales Corporation,
257 Park Avenue South, New York, NY 10010, USA.

Macmillan Distribution Services,
53 Park West Drive, Derrimut, Vic 3030, Australia.

To the Music Trade only:
Music Sales Limited,
8/9 Frith Street, London W1D 3JB, UK.

Photo credits:
Front cover: LFI
Back cover: Kevin Mazur / WireImage

All images LFI except:
Fotos International / Rex Features: 55; Bob Gruen / Starfile: 11 (below);
HWR / Rex Features: 79; Michel Linssen / Redferns: 24, 100;
Kevin Mazur / WireImage: 69, 71 (below); PVA / Rex Features: 45;
Brian Rasic / Rex Features: 23, 37 (below); Gene Shaw / Starfile: 13;
Sipa Press / Rex Features: 94, 97, 98 (top); Stephen Sweet / Rex Features: 72, 123;
TDY / Rex Features: 9, 10; Ian Tilton / Retna UK: 85 (below); VDL / Starfile: 128

Colour Picture Section Credits:
David Dyson / Camera Press: 7; Youri Lenquette / Retna: 1; LFI: 2, 3, 4, 5;
Kevin Mazur / WireImage: 6; Ralph Perou / NME / Camera Press: 8

Every effort has been made to trace the copyright holders of the
photographs in this book but one or two were unreachable.
We would be grateful if the photographers concerned would contact us.

Printed by: Caligraving Limited, Thetford, Norfolk.

A catalogue record for this book is available from the British Library.

Visit Omnibus Press on the web at www.omnibuspress.com

CONTENTS

Kurt Cobain was obsessed with the truth, and Courtney Love is *never* at a loss for words. Between them they filled up hundreds of column inches in magazines throughout the world. But honesty is not always the best policy in rock, and if Kurt and Courtney had been a shade more economical with the truth, then their relationship with the press – and the public image that resulted from this relationship – would have taken on an altogether different focus.

Showcased and heralded in the music press in their infancy, both Nirvana and Hole benefited from early, essential press exposure. It was a mutually beneficial relationship, with Nirvana helping to sell magazines and magazines helping to sell Nirvana.

Introduction

But by the end of Kurt's life, and well into Courtney Love's career with Hole, both had taken a dramatic U-turn against the press, claiming they had been used, abused, betrayed, misquoted, misrepresented and above all seriously damaged by inaccurate press reporting. This was the same press that had once been so good to them. The drama culminated with *Vanity Fair*'s notorious and extremely damaging article centred on Courtney Love's behaviour during her pregnancy which provoked an incensed Kurt Cobain to claim the press had unjustly portrayed him as a whinging, egotistical, drug-addicted rock-star.

Kurt and Courtney then began to treat the press with outspoken contempt. The media, to say the least, was not impressed. They themselves felt used. The press felt Kurt and Courtney had enjoyed the carefree cartoon punk characterisations both had helped to create and now, overtaken by their own success, had the audacity to turn around and blame the press for their misfortune.

Kurt and Courtney felt they had been thrust unwillingly under a microscope for the whole world to see. Soon the dreaded words 'responsibility' and 'role-model' began to rear their heads everywhere and the Cobains came to the conclusion they had sold themselves to the devil. The nightmare they had always feared was turning into a reality before their very eyes.

Kurt Cobain remains the James Dean of modern-day rock – the man who lived fast, died young and left a world-famous corpse. Courtney, meanwhile, has seen her musical and cinematic exploits battle for publicity with transatlantic airliner incidents, removing items of clothing at every appropriate opportunity, making a stand against corporate record-company greed and guarding her late husband's musical legacy by whatever means necessary.

Kurt and Courtney were the glamour couple of grunge, the names on everyone's lips... ten years later, the talking has yet to stop.

INTRODUCTION

Aspirations & Exasperations

> "You didn't have to do anything to be considered extreme back there. Just take a lot of acid." **KURT ON ABERDEEN, HIS HOME TOWN, 1991**

> **"I always wanted to move to the big city. I wanted to move to Seattle, find a chicken hawk (*slang for Suger Daddy*), sell my ass, and be a punk rocker, but I was too afraid. So I just stayed in Aberdeen for too long, until I was 20 years old."** KURT, 1992

> "When I was about twelve I wanted to be a rock n' roll star, and I thought that would be my payback to all the jocks who got girlfriends all the time. But I realised way before I came a rock star that was stupid." **KURT, 1992**

> **"The cheerleaders thought I was cute. The jocks would try to befriend me because they knew the jock-girls thought I was cute. Just chose not to hang around with them. It was really fun to fuck with people all the time."** KURT ON HIGH SCHOOL

> "I felt alienated, I started feeling confused. I couldn't understand why I didn't want to hang out with the kids at school. Years later I realised why - I didn't relate to them because they didn't appreciate anything artistic or cultural." **KURT**

> **"I always wanted to experience the street life because my teenage life in Aberdeen was so boring. But I was never really independent enough to do it. I applied for food stamps, I lived under the bridge, and built a fort at a cedar mill. I eventually moved to Olympia. And until I met The**

Melvins, my life was really boring. All of a sudden, I found a totally different world. I started getting into music and finally seeing shows and doing the things I always wanted to do while I was in High School.**"**

KURT, 1992

"I was always more of a feminine person when I was young. I just didn't know it. Then, when my hormones started swinging around and I started to get facial hair, I had to let off my male steam somewhere. So I started smoking pot and listening to Black Sabbath and Black Flag. It took The Pixies to put me on the right track and off the whole macho punk rock trip.**"** KURT, 1992

"I was moved around a lot. I have a really dysfunctional family. My mother is real detached. My real father is insane. The only good person in my family is my stepfather. He wasn't in my life that much, though, and I was in juvenile hall for four years, boarding school for three years. You know I tried to be a stoner because they were bad. I felt really lonely. I was weird. But then I discovered Patti Smith. She saved my life." COURTNEY, 1992

"I was tired of pretending I was someone else just to get along with people, just for the sake of having friendships. I was wearing flannel shirts and chewing tobacco, and so I became a monk in my room for years. And I forgot what it was like to socialise.**"**

KURT, 1992

ASPIRATIONS & **EXASPERATIONS**

"I had a really good childhood up until I was nine years old. Then a classic case of divorce really affected me and I moved back and forth between relatives all the time. And I just became extremely depressed and withdrawn." KURT, 1992

"I grew up in alternative families. I grew up in extended families. I grew up living with my therapist and my step-brother and my mother's ex-lover and on and on and I just think it sucks. This is just a personal preference. I think when you get married, it should be forever. Even though I did get married once and it was annulled. I don't know. For myself, I just want to have kids by the same person and stay with the same person.**"** **COURTNEY, 1992**

"I almost came out Republican the way I was raised. I mean, I was raised by white trash that considered themselves hippies. But to me, a mom and a dad is a really important thing to have."

COURTNEY, 1992

"I was a seriously depressed kid. Every night at one point I'd go to bed bawling my head off. I used to try to make my head explode by holding my breath, thinking if I blew up my head, they'd be sorry... I wanted to die. I wanted to kill. I wanted to smash things.**"**

KURT, 1993

"I never wanted to sing. I just wanted to play rhythm guitar, hide in the back and just play. But during those high-school years when I was playing guitar in my bedroom, I at least had the intuition that I had to write my own songs." KURT, 1994

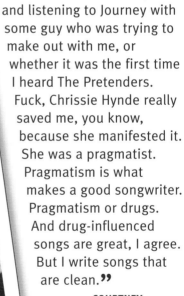

66Stripping's alright. It's better than prostitution. I was lucky, because I was fat. So nobody paid any attention to me. It was a totally normal thing to do: every girl in a band did it so they could buy guitars and amps.99 COURTNEY

66I felt alienated, I started feeling confused. I couldn't understand why I didn't want to hang out with the kids at school. Years later I realised why – I didn't relate to them because they didn't appreciate anything artistic or cultural. In Aberdeen, 99% of people had no idea what music was. Or art. It was there bread to become loggers. And I was such a small kid, really small, which was why I didn't want to go into the logging industry.99 KURT

66Well, I'm jaded. I've faced every situation for many years with a certain naivete and innocence. But I've somehow become a cynic. Cynicism is a good thing to have on the outside, but it's a terrible thing to have on the inside. All I ever wanted, ever, was to make rock music. Whether it was in the back of a Camaro smoking pot and listening to Journey with some guy who was trying to make out with me, or whether it was the first time I heard The Pretenders. Fuck, Chrissie Hynde really saved me, you know, because she manifested it. She was a pragmatist. Pragmatism is what makes a good songwriter. Pragmatism or drugs. And drug-influenced songs are great, I agree. But I write songs that are clean.99

COURTNEY, 1994

ASPIRATIONS & **EXASPERATIONS** 99

"Every parent made the same mistake. I don't know exactly what it is, but my story is exactly the same as 90% of everyone my age. Everyone's parents got divorced, their kids smoked pot all through high school, they grew up during the era when there was a massive Communist threat and everyone thought we were going to die from nuclear war, and more and more violence started to infuse into our society, and everyone's reaction is the same. And everyone's personalities are practically the same. There's just a handful of people my age, there's maybe five different personalities and they're all kind of intertwined with one another. I don't think our musical version of that is any different than any of the other band that have come out at the same time we have."

KURT, 1994

"Guys in stripey pants in a circle around me, and my mother telling me to act like spring. People in tents with wild eyes, painting my face. I remember a really big house in San Francisco and all my father's exotic girlfriends. We went to Oregon pretty quick, then things got a little more straightened out. Mother remarried and went to college in Eugene." **COURTNEY, RECALLING HER CHILDHOOD**

"A lot of it – I believe in my heart – is a projection that my mother made on me because of a repulsion she felt for my father, for which I don't blame her. But it is something that she denies to the death. If I had a child and I was repulsed by the father I would have a difficult time. Knowing the history of my father, I don't know if I would try and make up for it."

COURTNEY, ON HER RELATIONSHIP WITH HER MOTHER

"First it's Love Michelle Harrison, then it's Courtney Michelle Harrison, then it's Courtney Michelle Rodriguez, then it's Manely, then, finally, it's Courtney Love."

COURTNEY, ON ARRIVING AT HER PRESENT NAME, 1995

"I was really quite pretty until I was 11 or 12, which I think the back of *Live Through This* shows. I sort of looked like Eddie Vedder. I was the last girl on the planet with tits. I was the girl that would never hit puberty. I forever looked like I was seven. And then I got ugly; I was ugly until I was 25. But back then, I was usually one of the most attractive people in the room, except in an unusual way. Still I knew what I had, and I worked the fuck out of it. and so when it was gone I really missed it. I really resented puberty for that. It took away my beauty.** COURTNEY, 1995

There were all these hairy, wangly-ass hippies in our house. We had this huge mansion in Marcola, Oregon, and all these hippies are doing Gestalt therapy, running around the swimming pool naked, screaming. My mom was also adamant about a gender-free household: no dresses, no patent leather shoes, no canopy beds, nothing. **COURTNEY, ON HER CHILDHOOD HOME LIFE, 1995**

I started getting fascinated with the local coterie of juvenile delinquent girls. I'd been living in New Zealand, I'm really into the Rollers, I had a semi-David Bowie hairdo, and I'm a freak at my school. I get the shit beaten out of me enough times so I start to become real scrappy. I was a runt – no tits, no period, no puberty – so I get picked on, and I realise that I can fight really well if I pretend I'm going to murder the person. I started hanging around the mall and running with this crowd of teen whores.

COURTNEY, ON HOW SHE PICKED UP HER NOW-LEGENDARY FIGHTING SKILLS, 1995

KURT & **COURTNEY** *Talking*

Seattle & Grunge

❝We're getting fed up with this backwoods image kind of thing we're getting. It's like, you know there's an Aberdeen in every state in the US which is redneck, hillbilly. We're not unique.❞ **KURT, 1991**

❝**Every time somebody says the word 'Seattle,' you have to say 'Nirvana'. People are sick of us. More people probably hate us in Seattle than anywhere else in the country.**❞ KRIST NOVOSELIC, 1992

❝It's easier to get drugs in Seattle than in Los Angeles. The availability of drugs on Capitol Hill (Seattle) is disgusting.❞

COURTNEY, 1994

❝**Grunge is as potent a term as New Wave. You can't get out of it. It's going to be passe. You have to take a chance and hope that either a totally different audience accepts you or the same audience grows with you.**❞ KURT, 1994

❝I didn't really talk until I started hanging out in '80 or '81 with the drag queens at the Metropolis (a new wave gay club) in Portland. I was very, very quiet. So much so that at one point when I was very young I was diagnosed as a probable autistic. And then I started hanging out with bitchy drag queens and they basically raised me. I found my inner-bitch and ran with her.❞ **COURTNEY, 1995**

❝**You do something for me, and I'll do something for you. Throw that Pearl Jam T-shirt on stage and I'll play 'Pennyroyal Tea'. I want you all to do something for Kurt. I want you to take your Pearl Jam records and take your Nirvana records and separate them wide apart. I want you to do that for Kurt. Kurt is watching you.**❞ COURTNEY, 1995

Musical Influences

❝I blame *Sandinista* for not letting me get into punk, years after I should have done. It was so bad.❞ **KURT, 1991**

❝**We saw Shonen Knife and they were so cool. I turned into a nine-year-old girl at a Beatles concert. I was crying and jumping up and down and tearing my hair out – it was amazing. I've never been so thrilled in my whole life. They played pop music – pop, pop, pop, music.**❞ KURT, 1992

❝We (Nirvana) wanted to do as good as Sonic Youth. We totally respect those people and what they've done. We thought we'd sell a couple of thousand records at the most, and that would be fine. Next thing you know, we go Top 10. I wish we could have a time machine and go back to two months ago. I'd tell people to get lost.❞ **KRIST NOVOSELIC, 1992**

❝**I got really depressed. I moved back to Portland and I was just going to be a stripper for the rest of my life and never have a band again. But I heard Mudhoney's 'Touch Me I'm Sick' one night, and I was saved. I knew that I could scream on cue like that.**❞ COURTNEY, ON HER DECISION TO GIVE UP STRIPPING IN FAVOUR OF
PURSUING A MUSICAL CAREER

❝We (Nirvana) grew up on power ballads. We grew up on AM radio and AM radio is nothing more than melodic bullshit – The Carpenters, Tony Orlando and Dawn, stuff like that.❞
KURT COBAIN. 1992

"I got to sit and listen to this man serenade me. He told me The Meat Puppets' second record was great. I couldn't stand it. Then he played it to me – in his voice, his cadence, his timing. And I realised he was right." COURTNEY, 1994

"I was trying to write the ultimate pop song ('Teen Spirit'). I was basically trying to rip-off The Pixies. I have to admit it. When I heard The Pixies for the first time, I connected with that band so heavily I should have been in that band or at least in a Pixies cover band. We used their sense of dynamics, being soft and quiet and then loud and hard." KURT, 1994

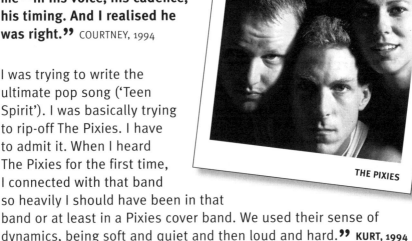

THE PIXIES

"I think that Debbie Harry's a very nice person, and I think that she had a really droll delivery and was cool, and I loved her attitude, but she's not one of my role models. Obviously, Madonna's not a role model of mine... Madonna or anybody who's that sexual." COURTNEY

"John Lennon was definitely my favourite Beatle, hands down. I don't know who wrote what parts of what Beatles songs, but Paul McCartney embarrasses me. Lennon was obviously disturbed. So I could relate to that." KURT, 1994

"I totally get in arguments with people about Paul (McCartney). I could do it for hours, the merits of Paul. Like if there was no Paul there would be no 'Helter Skelter'. If there had been no 'Helter Skelter' there would be no Sonic Youth. That's true. This is a really good ancient argument of ours. Kurt always goes: 'Oh? Who played the chords?' 'I don't care. Paul wrote the song. No one sticks up for Paul. Actually, there's a real Paul song on our record, called 'Miss World'." COURTNEY

MUSICAL INFLUENCES

“All the albums that I ever liked were albums that delivered a great song, one after another: Aerosmith's *Rocks*, The Sex Pistols' *Never Mind The Bollocks*, *Led Zeppelin II*, *Back In Black* by AC/DC.**”**

KURT, 1994

“If I could write just a couple of songs as good as what they (R.E.M.) have written... I don't know how that band does what they do. God, they're the greatest. They've dealt with their success like saints, and they keep delivering good music.” KURT

“I would love to write a couple of great rock songs in my life, like Chrissie Hynde did. She's really the only person of my gender who I find completely accomplished, because as much as I love Patti Smith, she didn't write her own music.**”** COURTNEY, 1993

“To put 'About A Girl' on *Bleach* was a risk. I was heavily into pop, I really liked R.E.M., and I was into all kinds of old Sixties' stuff. But there was a lot of pressure within that social scene, the underground – like the type of thing you get in high-school. And to put a jangly R.E.M. type of pop song on a grunge record, in that scene, was risky.”

KURT, 1994

“All in all we sound like The Knack and The Bay City Rollers being molested by Black Flag and Black Sabbath.**”** KURT

R.E.M.

Songwriting

"As time goes on, my songs are getting poppier and poppier as I get happier and happier. The songs are now about conflicts in relationships, emotional things with other human beings. We're writing a lot more pop songs, like 'About A Girl' on *Bleach*. Some people might think of that as 'changing' into something, but it's something that we've always been aware of and are just now starting to express." **KURT, 1989**

"I started working on songwriting right away when I got a guitar, rather than learn a bunch of Van Halen covers. I had to develop my own style. I only know a couple of cover songs to this day, and they're the ones I learned when I first had the guitar – 'My Best Friend's Girl' by The Cars and Zeppelin's 'Communication Breakdown'." KURT

"When I write a song, the lyrics are the least important thing. I can go through two or three different subjects in a song, and the title can mean absolutely nothing at all." **KURT, 1989**

"It's not hard to keep your dignity and sign to a major label. Sonic Youth have been really smart about what they're doing. I feel we're experienced enough to deal with it now. We're changing a little, we've been into more accessible pop styles of music for the last two years, and finally we're being able to relieve ourselves of some of that. So we figured we may as well get on the radio and try to make a bit of money at it." KURT COBAIN, 1990

"We've never known how many records we've sold at Sub-Pop. We don't know how many copies of *Bleach* we sold. And we weren't being promted very well. I challenge anyone to find a *Bleach* ad."

KURT, EXPLAINING NIRVANA'S CONTROVERSIAL DECISION TO DEFECT FROM THE INDEPENDENTLY OWNED SUB-POP LABEL TO GEFFEN

KURT & **COURTNEY** *Talking*

❝I think of my new songs as pop songs, as they're arranged with the standard pop format: verse, chorus, verse, chorus, solo, bad solo. There won't be any songs as heavy as 'Paper Cuts' or 'Sifting' on the new record. That's just too boring. I'd rather have a good hook.❞ KURT ON THE DEVELOPMENT OF *NEVERMIND*, 1990

❝We approached the recording of *Bleach* like it was a radio session. The key to a successful album is to get the fuck out of the studio before you're sick of the songs. I hate *Bleach* so much now.❞

KURT, 1991

❝A lot of it is just narrative. I mean, Neil Young writes narrative and nobody thinks... well, you know what I mean. The songs still feel like catharsis, still feels like exorcism, still feel really good to sing, but, on the other hand, a lot of it is just narrative. I'm not a character actress, I'm a songwriter.❞ COURTNEY ON HER LYRICS, 1991

❝Antique craftsmanship, something that is built well, to last, something solid. Values that my grandparents had – pretty much the opposite of the way things are going now. It's the same with music – sincerity, craftsmanship. If you do a job, you should do it well – that's just good business sense. Same thing my grandfather used to bitch at me about when I was a kid, and I never understood him.❞

COURTNEY ON SONGWRITING

"It's about a young girl who was abducted. The guy drove her around in his van. Tortured her. Raped her. The only chance she had of getting away was to come on to him and persuade him to untie her. That's what she did, and she got away. Can you imagine how much strength that took?" KRIST NOVOSELIC DESCRIBING THE TRUE TO LIFE STORY THAT IS THE BASIS BEHIND THE LYRICS TO NIRVANA'S 'POLLY'

"Our songs are about changing yourself, frustration. There was this anthem the skate-rock kids were claiming for their own, 'Don't Resist', to not resist against repression. 'No Recess', one of our new songs, was just some surreal idea I had about being in school and being in social cliques all the time, and then you grow-up, having to deal with exactly the same things with your friends at parties and in clubs as you did in high school. It's exactly the same.**"** KURT, 1991

"Mom and dad go off somewhere and leave the kid with his grandparents and he doesn't understand what's happening to him. But hey, you mustn't get too worried about him – grandpa doesn't abuse him or anything like that. And in the last verse he wakes up back in his mother's arms." KURT EXPLAINING THE LYRICS BEHIND THE SONG 'SLIVER' WHICH APPEARED ON BOTH *BLEACH* AND *INCESTICIDE*, 1991

"And let me just state one last thing. And that this last record (*Pretty On The Inside*), it was really bilious and black-hearted in a lot of ways. But we have a lot of shit in us as well, you know, and... But I'm really getting into songwriting as a craft, so maybe our next album will be more like a tribute to The Beach Boys. Or maybe not. But I do know that we are still evolving, and that there's a pop consciousness out there that I really don't know anything about.**"**
COURTNEY, 1991

"We're definitely not groundbreaking. If there was no Sub Pop sound we'd still be doing this. If there's anything we're really close to, it's The Stooges – the momentum and the energy." KRIST NOVOSELIC TRYING TO EXPLAIN THE NIRVANA SOUND, 1991

SONGWRITING

Handwritten in left margin: Cut, cut, Cut the surface yet that's not enough until you reach the end - 2/7/13

❝Most of the music is really personal as far as the emotion and the experiences that I've had in my life, but most of the themes in the songs aren't that personal. They're more just stories from TV or books or movies or friends. But definitely the emotion and feeling is from me.❞ **KURT, 1992**

❝*Bleach* **was recorded for (about) $600 on eight tracks. We recorded in three days, hacked it in, hacked it out. The sense of urgency shows through. On** *Nevermind***, we were lucky in this studio from the Seventies. It was like a time machine. It was like an old pair of corduroys that was starting to wear out. Just like a studio Abba would have recorded in. We'd just stagger in late, then get intense with it.❞** KRIST NOVOSELIC ON *BLEACH*, 1992

❝I was looking for something a lot heavier, yet melodic at the same time. Something different from heavy metal, a different attitude.❞

KURT, 1992

❝**It's about breath smells and underarm deodorant.❞**

KURT ON 'SMELLS LIKE TEEN SPIRIT', 1992

❝People think I'm a moody person, and I think it's lame that there are only two kinds of male singer. You can either be a moody visionary like Michael Stipe, or a mindless heavy metal party guy like Sammy Hagar. I guess it's better to be called a moody visionary than a mindless party animal. I tried to become an alcoholic once, but it didn't work.❞ **KURT, 1992**

❝**We downed a lot of hypodermic cough syrup and Jack Daniel's and just lounged on the couch in the recreation area of the studio for days on end, just writing down a few lyrics here and there. If we hadn't met our time commitments at the end of our recording period, we would just have bought our songs from Gloria Estefan or Warrant or J Mascis. J's got a shit-load of songs floating around. He's always trying to palm them off on people too... 'Here, you wanna' buy a song for a quarter?' We can afford that 'cos we're on a major label now.❞** KURT ON *NEVERMIND*, 1992

❝I did allow the record (*Nevermind*) to be produced cleaner and more commercial than I wanted it to be. I don't know what the reasoning for that was, besides just being dead tired of hearing the same songs. We'd tried remixing it three times and we rang this professional mixologist to do it and, by that point, I was so tired of hearing the songs, I said, 'Go ahead, do whatever you want'.❞

KURT, 1993

❝**The same thing happened in the punk movement when it happened in the late Seventies. Major record labels were signing punk bands shortly after most punk bands first gig, they would be starting their first gig and would be signing to major labels right away, just because it's a trend right now and that just proves that there are a lot of old school Dinosaurs in the music industry that need to be weeded out.**❞ KURT

❝We spent two weeks in Minnesota recording some of the best tracks we've ever done, and most of the mixes from that session are perfect. However Steve (Albini) would not spend much time on

the mixes and overall we – the band – felt the vocals were not loud enough on a few of the tracks. We want to change that. **99 KURT'S PRESS RELEASE FOR WHY THE FINAL MIX OF *IN UTERO* WAS TAKING SO LONG**

66 Steve(Albini) has made a career about being anti-commercial or anti-establishment. But being commercial or anti-commercial is not what makes a good rock record. It's the songs, and until we have the songs the way we want them Nirvana will not release this record. 99 KURT ON ALBINI'S PRODUCTION FOR *IN UTERO*, 1993

66 I think there are a few songs on *In Utero* that could have been cleaned up a little more. Definitely 'Pennyroyal Tea'. That was not recorded right. There's something wrong with that. That should have been recorded like *Nevermind*, because that's a strong song, a hit single. **99 KURT ON THE PRODUCTION PROBLEMS WITH *IN UTERO***

66 Obviously, though they never said it, they (the record company) wanted us to re-record, or at least remix, but at the time I couldn't really say much to anyone because I wasn't sure myself what I wanted to change on the album. The first time I played it at home, I knew there was something wrong. The whole first week I wasn't really interested in listening to it at all, and that usually doesn't happen. I just got no emotion from it, and that usually doesn't happen. I got no emotion from it, I was just numb. So for three weeks Krist and Dave and I listened to the record every night, trying to figure out what was wrong with it, and we talked about it and decided the vocals weren't loud enough, the bass was inaudible and you couldn't hear the lyrics. That was about it. We knew we couldn't possibly re-record because we knew we'd achieved the sound that we wanted – the basic sound was typical Steve Albini, which was the sound we really wanted bad. So we decided to remix two of favourite tracks, just as a litmus test, and we left it at that because to remix anymore would have destroyed the ambience of the whole thing. We decided to take a chance on mastering, which we really didn't understand. We thought it was the last stage in the process where you just take the tapes in and run them through a machine that allows you to cut it onto a record, or whatever. So we went to the

SONGWRITING

mastering plant and learnt that you can actually take the vocals right out, if you want to. It's amazing. So that's what we did, we just gave the bass more high-end so you could hear the notes, turned the vocals up, maybe compressed it a little, and that did it, cured everything. As soon as we'd done it, we knew we'd made the right decision, it was over. And now I wouldn't change anything on it, I'm 100 per cent satisfied.**"** KURT ON THE CONTROVERSIAL TOPIC OF THE (ALBINI) MIX AND SUBSEQUENT REMIXING OF *IN UTERO*

"I was trying to write a song that supported women and dealt with the issue of rape. Over the last few years, people have had such a hard time understanding what our message is, what we're trying to convey, that I just decided to be as bold as possible. How hard should I stamp this point... how big should I make the letters? It's not a pretty image? But a women who's been raped, who is infuriated with the situation... it's like 'go ahead, rape me, just go for it because you're gonna' get it.' I'm a firm believer in karma, and that motherfucker is going to get what he deserves, eventually. That man will be caught, he'll go to jail, and he'll be raped. 'So rape me, do it, get it over with. Because you're gonna' get it worse.'**"** **KURT EXPLAINING THE MEANING BEHIND THE TITLE OF 'RAPE ME'**

"When I was making *Pretty On The Inside*, I had just been kicked out of Babes In Toyland, and I had a real chip on my shoulder. I was like, 'I'm going to be the angriest girl in the world, fuck you!' I didn't want to have a crack in my surface and put anything jangly on there. I really wish I had put something pretty on there. I mean I'm glad people don't expect much from me, but at the same time, I wish they had an inkling of how to write."

COURTNEY, 1993

"She was institutionalised numerous times and, in the place in Washington where she ended up, the custodians there had people lining up all the way through the halls, waiting to rape her. She had been beaten up and brutally raped for years, every day. She didn't even have clothes most of the time. Courtney especially could relate to Frances Farmer. I made the comparison between the two. When I was reading the book, I realised that this could very well happen to Courtney if things kept going on. There's only so much a person can take, you know? I've been told by doctors and psychiatrists that public humiliation is one of the most extreme and hardest things to heal yourself from. It's as bad as being brutally raped, or witnessing one of your parents murdered in front of your eyes or something like that. It just goes on and on, it grinds into you and it's so personal. And the Frances Farmer thing was a massive conspiracy involving the bourgeois and powerful people in Seattle, especially this one judge who still lives in Seattle to this day. He led this crusade to so humiliate her that she would go insane. In the beginning, she was hospitalised – totally against her will – and she wasn't even crazy. She got picked up on a drunk driving charge and got committed, you know. It was a very scary time to be confrontational." **KURT COBAIN EXPLAINING WHO FRANCES FARMER WAS AND WHY HE WROTE A SONG DEDICATED TO HER**

"I just simply wanted to remind people of tragedies like that. It's very real and it can happen. People can be driven insane, they can be given lobotomies and be committed and be put in jails for no reason. I mean, from being this glamorous, talented, well respected movie star, she ended up being given a lobotomy and working in a Four Seasons restaurant."
KURT ON FRANCES FARMER

SONGWRITING

" That's just about people who're easily amused, people who not only aren't capable of progressing their intelligence but are totally happy watching 10 hours of television and really enjoy it. I've met a lot of dumb people. They have a shitty job, they might be totally lonely, they don't have a girlfriend, they don't have much of a social life, and yet for some reason, they're happy... I wish I could take a pill that would allow me to be amused by television and just enjoy the simple things in life, instead of being so judgmental and expecting real good quality instead of shit. The songs not about me, but it *has* been. And just using the word 'Happy' I thought was a nice twist on the negative stuff we've done before. **"**

KURT ON THE SONG 'DUMB', 1993

"Almost all my lyrics have been cut-ups, pieces of poetry and stuff. And the pieces of poetry are taken from poems that don't usually have meaning in the first place. They were cut-ups themselves. And often I'll have to obscure the pieces I take to make them fit in the song, so they're not even true pieces of poem." KURT, 1993

" I very rarely write about one theme or one subject. I end up getting bored with that theme and write something else halfway through the rest of the song, and finish the song with a different idea. **"**

COURTNEY, 1994

"It was made really fast. All the basic tracks were done within a week. And I did 80% of the vocals in one day, in about seven hours. I just happened to be on a roll. It was a good day for me, and I just kept going." KURT ON THE RECORDING OF *IN UTERO*, 1994

" I was trying to write the ultimate pop song ('Teen Spirit') I was basically trying to rip off The Pixies. I have to admit it (smiles). When I heard The Pixies for the first time, I connected with that band so heavily, I should have been in that band, or at least in a Pixies cover band. We used their sense of dynamics being soft and quiet, then loud and hard. 'Teen Spirit' was such a cliched riff. It was so close to a Boston riff or 'Louie, Louie'. When I came up with the guitar part, Krist looked at me and said, 'That's is so ridiculous'. I made the band play it for an hour and a half. **"** **KURT, 1994**

SONGWRITING

❝I guess I start with the verse and go on to the chorus. But I'm getting so tired with that formula. And it is a formula. And there's not much you can do with it. We've mastered that for our band. We're all growing pretty tired of it. It is a dynamic style. But I'm only using two of the dynamics. There are a lot more that I could be using. Krist, Dave and I have been working on this formula – this thing of going from quiet to loud – for so long that it is literally becoming boring for us. It's like 'OK, I have this riff. I'll play it quiet without a distortion box, while I'm singing the verse. And now let's turn on the distortion box and hit the drums harder'. I want to learn to go in between those things, go back and forth, almost become psychedelic in a way but with a lot more structure. It's a really hard thing to do, and I don't know if we're capable of it, as musicians.❞ KURT, 1994

❝Everyone has focused on that song ('Teen Spirit') so much. The reason it gets a big reaction is, people have seen it on MTV a million times. It's been pound into their brains. But I think there are so many other songs that I've written that are as good, if not better, than that song, like 'Drain You'. That's definitely as good as 'Teen Spirit'. I love the lyrics, and I never get tired of playing it. Maybe if it was as big as 'Teen Spirit', I wouldn't like it as much.❞

KURT, 1994

❝Punk rock should mean freedom, liking and accepting everything that you like and playing everything that you like as sloppy as you like, as long as its good and has passion.❞ KURT

❝Every album that we've done so far, we've always had one to three songs left over from our sessions. And they usually have been pretty good, ones that we really liked, so we always had something to rely on – a hit or something that was above average. So this next record (*In Utero*) is going to be really interesting, because I have nothing left. I'm starting from scratch for the first time. I don't know what we're going to do.❞ **KURT, 1994**

"We have failed in showing the lighter, more dynamic side of our band. The big guitar sound is what the kid's want to hear. We like playing that stuff, but I don't know how much longer I can scream at the top of my lungs every night for an entire year on tour."

KURT, 1994

"As literal as a joke can be. Nothing more than a joke. And that had a bit to do with why we decided to take it off. We knew people wouldn't get it; they'd take it too seriously. It was totally satirical, making fun of ourselves. I'm thought of as this prissy, complaining, freaked-out schizophrenic who wants to kill himself all the time. 'He isn't satisfied with anything'. And I thought it was a funny title. I wanted it to be the title of the album for a long time. But I knew the majority of people wouldn't understand it."

KURT COBAIN ON THE WORKING TITLE FOR *IN UTERO - I HATE MYSELF AND I WANT TO DIE* – AND THE SONG OF THE SAME TITLE, 1994

SONGWRITING

❝I've always worked really hard on my lyrics, even when my playing was for shit. So it's weird that when I try to work in different styles, to juxtapose ideas in a careful way that isn't pompous and Byronic, it's just taken as vulgar. The whole cliché of women being cathartic really pisses me off. You know, 'Oh, this is therapy for me. I'd die if I didn't write this'. Eddie Vedder says shit like that. Fuck you.❞ COURTNEY ON HER LYRICS, 1994

❝Most of the lyrics are just contradictions. I'll write a few sincere lines and then I will have to make fun of it with another line.❞ KURT

❝I don't like things too obvious because if it is obvious it gets really stale... we don't mean to be really cryptic or mysterious, I just think that lyrics that are different, weird and spacey paint a nice picture, and it's just the way I like art.❞ KURT

❝That record was me posing in a lot of ways. It was the truth, but it was also me catching up with all my hip peers who'd gone all indie on me, and who made fun of me for liking R.E.M. and The Smiths. I'd done the whole punk thing, sleeping on floors in piss and beer, and waking up with the guy with the fucking mohawk and the skateboards and the speed and the whole goddamned thing. But I hated it. I'd outgrown it by the time I was 17.❞

COURTNEY ON *PRETTY ON THE INSIDE*

"*Live Through This* was just me on three gears, not four. Because my fourth gear was sucked up through drugs, a relationship. I did not have a fourth gear to work with. The purity was not completely there. It was like where in school I would cram – not do my homework. If I did it, I know I'd get an A. I'd cram and get a B or B+. I never did that extra footwork for the A. This record was a B-. And I knew that was enough to get by-in terms of my peers." COURTNEY ON *LIVE THROUGH THIS*, 1994

"I just hope I don't become so blissful I become boring. I think I'll always be neurotic enough to do something weird.**"** **KURT, 1994**

"How's that for sick." COURTNEY REFLECTING ON THE SAD IRONY IN THE CHOICE OF TITLE OF HOLE'S ALBUM *(LIVE THROUGH THIS)* IN THE WAKE OF KURT'S SUICIDE

"I might lie a lot, but never in my lyrics.**"** **COURTNEY, 1995**

"'Violet' (on *Live Through This*) was officially born on Halloween at St. Andrews Hall in Detroit opening for the Laughing Hyenas with 40 people there. And I was in the van outside the show during sound check, and we had five songs from *Nevermind*, and I was so jealous of those songs that I had to try and top them. I could not believe that someone I knew, from our underground, had written a batch of songs that fiercely great." COURTNEY, 1995

"There was a time before I was in Hole when I was living in San Francisco and I had a real pop sensibility – I played the 'Peter Buck D chord' with the pinky. And in the first band, which was called Sugar Babylon, with Kat Bjelland and Jennifer Finch, Literally the verbatim was, 'You like R.E.M. too much. You wanna be R.E.M. too much' because I'd be listening to *Reckoning* all the time. And I was thrown out of Babes In Toyland and Faith No More for that exact reason.**"** **COURTNEY, 1999**

SONGWRITING

Each Other

66 Back then, we didn't have any emotion towards each other. It was like, 'Are you coming over to my house?' 'Are you going to get it up?' 'Fuck you'. That sort of thing. 99

COURTNEY ON HER EARLY RELATIONSHIP WITH KURT COBAIN

66 **We bonded over pharmaceuticals. I had Vicodin extra-strength, which was pills, and he had Hycomine cough syrup.** 99

COURTNEY, 1994

66 It's like Evian water and battery acid. And when you mix the two you get love. 99 **KURT ON THE CHEMISTRY BETWEEN COURTNEY AND HIMSELF.**

66 **I've always been comfortable about notoriety, but I feel like I married Bobby Sherman.** 99 COURTNEY

66 I'm just happier than I've
ever been. I finally found
someone that I'm totally
compatible with. It doesn't
matter whether she's
a male, female or
hermaphrodite or a donkey.
We're compatible. 99

KURT, 1992

66 **I'm not as much of a
neurotic, unstable person
as I was. I used to feel I
was always alone, even
though I had lots of
friends and a band that
I really enjoyed being**

with. Now I've found someone I'm close to, who's interested in the things I do, and I really don't have many other aspirations. KURT, 1992

"I'd heard about her, though – some nasty rumours, that she was this perfect replica of Nancy Spungen. That got my attention. Like everyone else, I loved Sid 'cos he was such a likeable, dopey guy. I've often felt that many people think of me as a stupid, impressionable person, so I thought that maybe going out with someone who was meant to be like Nancy would stick a thorn in everyone's side, 'cos it's the exact opposite of what they would want me to do. Courtney certainly helped me to put Nirvana in perspective; to realise that my reality doesn't entirely revolve around the band and that I can deal without it if I have to. Which doesn't mean I'm planning on breaking up the band, but that the minimal amount of success I strive for isn't of much importance anymore.**"** KURT, 1992

"Everyone seems to think that we couldn't possibly love each other, because we're thought of as cartoon characters, because we're public domain. So the feelings that we have for each other are thought of as superficial." KURT, 1992

"The fact that I judge myself on Kurt's terms is part of me subscribing to the whole male rock ethic, too. Kim Gordon – like every other woman I respected – told me that this marriage was going to be a disaster for me. They told me that I was more important than Kurt because I have this lyric thing going and I'm more culturally significant.**"** COURTNEY, 1993

EACH OTHER

❝The whole glamorous girlfriend idea... I've just said, fuck you to it from the beginning. When I first went out with my husband, *Pretty On The Inside* was outselling Nirvana's début album, *Bleach*, two to one. Anyone who's well informed knows that.❞

COURTNEY

❝I am the just the classic person who wants to learn stuff. I want good tutors, and with Kurt I had the best.❞ COURTNEY

❝There's this insane attitude about women which really fucks me and my plans up. All that shit about me and Kurt – 'She's just a money grabber gold digger bitch whore slut'. Let's get one thing straight: I adore him. I worship him. I went through all the shit and pain and inconvenience of being pregnant for nine whole fucking months because I wanted some of his beautiful genes in there, in that child. I wanted his babies. I saw something I wanted, and I got it. What's wrong with that? What is so fucking bad about getting what you want?❞ COURTNEY, 1994

❝Well Jesus, don't flatter him all at once. One minute he's a leader, a voice for a generation – next minute I'm spoon-feeding him cereal and fucking his life up. Kurt went after me. I wanna tell you about how we finally got together. Hang on a minute...❞ COURTNEY, 1994

❝Kurt and I couldn't collaborate until I'd proved myself. Then we could do whatever the fuck we want. I'm not going to be seen as Yoko. She was an avant-garde artist. At the time she didn't have a chance anyway, but she shouldn't have used her husband's power to help herself. I've always tried to stay away from that... I think

it's very baby boomer to put me in the position of being Sid and Nancy or John and Yoko, because we were neither. We were definitely our own couple."
COURTNEY, 1995

"Kurt looked upon time and marriage as an aphrodisiac. He looked upon stability as arousing. And he really cured me of my former cheating problem. Because my cheating problem had always been based on power. You know, like, 'Fuck you' power. And Kurt never played those games at all." **COURTNEY, 1995**

"When my husband was sitting in the studio, I could (concentrate on finishing *Live Through This*), 'cos' I knew where he was, so I didn't have to worry about him. But the worry factor was so much there for me... Kurt's vocals are on every track, practically, but they're buried. He just came to show me some harmonies then it was, well, keep some of mine... I have a printer on my computer so I can take all the lyrics Kurt ever wrote, as they were, and keep them somewhere, and take all the lyrics I ever wrote, as they are, and keep them somewhere, and divide them into, like, food/sex metaphors, complete suicidal misery metaphors, death/sex metaphors, whatever." COURTNEY, 1995

Kurt's Nirvana...

"Our (Nirvana's) big goal was to play in Seattle one day.**"** **KURT**

"I feel like we've (Nirvana) been tagged as illiterate redneck cousin-fucking kids. That's not true at all." KURT, 1988

"After the first practice, we knew that things were going to work out, because we had the same ideas. They wanted a drummer that played really big drums and hit extremely hard, so things worked out from there. And now Kurt has someone that can sing back-up vocals to the songs.**"** **DAVE GROHL ON HIS JOINING NIRVAVA AFTER DAN PETER'S RETURN TO MUDHONEY**

KRIST NOVOSELIC

"See Kurt had this tape, right. And we're living in Aberdeen and he made it with Dale, the drummer of The Melvins. That was in '86, maybe. I heard it and I thought it was really cool, so I said to start this band, so we started a band and we went through three drummers and we're here today, talking to you."

KRIST NOVOSELIC, 1991

"When I joined the band I lived with Kurt for eight months. When I first got there, he had just broken up with a girl and was completely heartbroken. We would sit in his tiny shoe box apartment for eight hours at a time without saying a word. For weeks and weeks this happened. Finally one night we were driving back in the van, and Kurt said, 'You know, I'm not always like this'. And I just went, 'Whewww'. **"**

DAVE GROHL, 1992

DAVE GROHL

"I think Kurt has something no one else has. His way of writing simple, childlike, minimalist tunes that stick. But that just shows you that you don't have to be so accomplished to impress. Anybody can do Kurt Cobain, anybody can do Krist Novoselic... I dunno. None of us were cut out for this." DAVE GROHL, 1992

"I don't even care about the band as much as I used to. I know that sounds shitty, but the band used to be the only thing that was important to me in my life, and now, I have a wife and a child. I still love the band, but it isn't the only thing I'm living for.**"** KURT, 1992

"It starts with Kurt, who might have a riff, and he'll bring it into the studio and start playing it. Chris and I will just start following along. We'll jam on it until verses and choruses pop up out of it. It's usually just jamming, there is no actual composing or writing." DAVE GROHL RECALLING *NEVERMIND*'S CREATION

"At the time I was writing those songs, I really didn't know what I was trying to say. There's no point in my even trying to analyse or explain it.**"**

KURT ON THE MEANING BEHIND CERTAIN SONGS ON *NEVERMIND*

KURT'S NIRVANA... & **COURTNEY'S HOLE**

"This is the hardest job I've ever had. I like it though. I'm thoroughly enjoying myself... it's just a lot more demanding than I expected." KURT, 1992

"I've gotten a bit more of a percentage on the songwriting royalties. I get a little bit more than Krist and Dave do because I write 99 per cent of the songs. I just felt entitled to it, you know... It took a bit of convincing on my part. I still believe in all-for one, one-for-all, you know. We're a group, we're a three-piece. Krist and Dave are equally as important as far as the persona of the band goes, in the way we're perceived. We're perceived as a *band* . But I had written 99% of the songs and many were the times when I've taken Krists' bass away from him and shown him what to play, and sat behind Dave's drumkit and shown *him* what to play, stuff like that. I don't enjoy being in that sort of dictatorship position, but I came up with the songs at home and introduced the songs to the band and I could be asking for a lot more... We still split the touring money, and the royalties off the record, and stuff like that. It's only an extra few thousand dollars a year or something. But it was a touchy subject at the time. I felt really guilty about asking for it. I just feel I'm entitled to it.**"**

KURT ON WHAT WAS LATER REVEALED OUT TO BE A 'VERY TOUCHY' SUBJECT THROUGHOUT NIRVANA'S EXISTENCE

"I ask their opinions about things. But ultimately, it's my decision. I always feel weird saying that; it feels egotistical. But we've never argued. Dave, Krist and I have never screamed at each other. Ever. It's not like they're afraid to bring up anything. I always ask their opinion, and we talk about it. And eventually we all come to the same conclusions." KURT, 1994

" Every time I look back at the best times in this band it was right before *Nevermind* came out. It was awesome. That's when the band is at its best – they're trying really hard and there's so much excitement in the air you can taste it. " KURT

" When I was doing drugs, it (band relations) was pretty bad. There was no communication. Krist and Dave, they didn't understand the drugs problem. They'd never been around drugs. They thought of heroin in the same way that I thought of heroin before I started doing it. It was just really sad. We didn't speak very often. They were thinking the worst, like most people would, and I don't blame them for that. But nothing is ever as bad as it seems. Since I've been clean, it's gone back to pretty much normal. " KURT, 1994

" I get all the lyrics. The music I get 75%, and they get the rest. I think that's fair. But at the time, I was on drugs when that came up. And so they thought that I might start asking for more things. They were afraid that I was going to go out of my mind and start putting them on a salary, stuff like that. But even then we didn't yell at each other. And we split everything else evenly. " KURT, 1994

KURT'S NIRVANA... & **COURTNEY'S HOLE** ""

...& Courtney's Hole

> He had a Thurston (Moore) quality about him. He was tall, skinny, blond. He dressed pretty cool, and he knew who Sonic Youth were. **COURTNEY LOVE ON WHY SHE IMMEADIATLY HIRED ERIC ERLANDSON AS HOLE'S GUITARIST, 1995**

> **Eric has come into his own at long last. He is a brilliant and respected guitarist. My bond with him has always been strange and twisted; we both want the same thing but go about getting it differently. I draw outside the lines and all the grown-ups think I'm super-original, while Eric traces that li'l deer in the back of the mag perfectly. So we connect in our weirdo way, and when we do, it's great, the very real truth, purity.** COURTNEY, 1995

> Hole operates under a democracy; one journalist tried desperately to paint us as three people trying to cover up for their alcoholic mom, but it's just not like that. I could never stomach the idea of being 'solo', although I admire others who can. Hell, I never even wanted to sing. When I was a teen, I wanted to be a great guitarist. But then I found myself onstage in innumerable bad bands, the only one drunk enough or, as Madonna put it at the Video Music Awards, 'in dire need of attention' enough to do it.
> Singing's easy once you let it out; when that primal roar came through me the first time I was electrified. **COURTNEY, 1995**

"We're not slackers. The people of this generation who are the slackers are the ones that come from the middle-class backgrounds rather than the hippy backgrounds. Our value system is, go away and do it until it's done, because we saw our parents half-finish the painting one too many times." COURTNEY, 1995

" Melissa Auf Der Maur. She's 22 and going through a little phase, being the cutest bass player in indie rock and knowing it. I loved watching all the boys throw themselves at her feet. Oh well.

HOLE: ERIC ERLANDSON, MELISSA AUF DER MAUR, COURTNEY & PATTY SCHEMEL

I always have the space for a charismatic brilliant bassist. Melissa arranged 'Sugar Coma', the best song we've ever, ever written in terms of tempo. Sometimes I feel guilty for loving Melissa's talent so much; it doesn't mean that I don't miss Kristen (Pfaff).**"**

COURTNEY, 1995

KURT'S NIRVANA... & **COURTNEY'S HOLE**

"I dived into the crowd (at a Hole gig) and the first thing some guy did was grab my tits." COURTNEY, 1995

"You can't deal with people screaming at you, shithead. Think what it's like for me. He wears the pants in this band, I swear.**"** **COURTNEY ON ERLANDSON, 1995**

"The Spanish and Italians were out of control; they love the loud blonde American thing. But the French just stood there. Eric (Erlandson) thinks it's because I'm just too tragic for them now." COURTNEY, 1995

MELISSA AUF DER MAUR AND COURTNEY

"I refused at that time to make the widow record. As much as I loved him and he was the best friend I ever had, I truly hate the stigma of having been married to him.**"**

COURTNEY ON THE MAKING OF HOLE'S 1998 ALBUM *CELEBRITY SKIN*, 2001

"I built that album, *Celebrity Skin*, as a monument. That important record where art and commerce are meeting, where discipline and restraint are meeting total organic truth. Like *Nevermind*. Like *Appetite For Destruction*. Like *Rumours*. Big, huge records with something to say." COURTNEY, 1998

"We'll get shit for the commerciality and the massiveness of this record (*Celebrity Skin*) but I don't care. We'll have grabbed a voice. And we'll have shown that somebody from where we're from can grab a voice and then... then... it'll change the fuckin' world.**"**

COURTNEY, 1999

"Hole had the record company by the fuckin' balls! And d'you know how we got 'em by the balls? It's kinda pathetic but I was gonna die... so like, what were they gonna do?" COURTNEY, 1998

"I heard last night that (Hole's record label) actually brought in a counsellor. They're the most detached, cold people in the world but they brought in a counsellor to counsel the staff when we were touring and I was all fucked up. They brought in a counsellor to teach the staff how to deal with me even though none of them ever did. It's a sick little business." COURTNEY, 1998

"On *Celebrity Skin*, what's really missing is my inner rhythm. Only this year did I learn that, like some little baby or second-rate band, the producer had put a click track not just on the drummer, but a slightly different one on the bassist, on Eric, and on me. That's like sabotage or rape – raping my rhythm. It's my own fault for allowing others to take responsibility for what I wrote and conceived and letting them have control. That won't happen again." COURTNEY, 2001

KURT'S NIRVANA... & **COURTNEY'S HOLE**

KURT & **COURTNEY** *Talking*

Drugs &
Their
Consequences

66 We (Kurt and I) went on a binge. We did a lot of drugs. We got pills and then we went down to Alphabet City and we copped some dope. Then we got high and did *Saturday Night Live*. After that, I did heroin for a couple of months. 99 **COURTNEY LOVE'S INFAMOUS STATEMENT TO** *VANITY FAIR*'**S LYNN HIRSCHBERG, TRIGGERING WIDESPREAD CONDEMNATION OF HER IRRESPONSIBLE BEHAVIOUR DURING PREGANCY**

66 **I don't even drink any more because it destroys my stomach. My body wouldn't allow me to take drugs if I wanted to, because I'm so weak. All drugs are a waste of time. They destroy your memory and your self-respect and everything that goes along with your self-esteem. They're no good at all. But I'm not going to go around preaching against it. It's your choice, but in my experience, I've found they're a waste of time.** 99 KURT, 1992

66 I have to hear rumours about me all the time. I'm totally sick of it. If I'm going to take drugs that's my own fucking prerogative, and if I don't take drugs it's my own fucking prerogative. It's nobody's business, and I don't care if people take drugs and I don't care if people don't take drugs. It all started with just one article in one of the shittiest, cock rock-oriented LA magazines; where this guy assumed I was on heroin because he noticed I was tired. Since then, the rumours have spread like wildflower. I can't deny that I have taken drugs and I still do every once in a while. But I'm not a fucking heroin addict. 99 **KURT, 1992**

"It's hard to believe that a person can put something as poisonous as alcohol or drugs in their system and the mechanics can take it – for a while." KURT

"I didn't do heroin during pregnancy. And even if I did, even if I shot coke every night and took acid every day, it's my own motherfucking business. If I'm amoral, I'm amoral. It's not your goddamn' business if I'm amoral or not." COURTNEY, 1992

"Yeah, it does get to me (continuous drug rumours), it pisses me off. I had no idea that being in a commercial rock band would be like this, because I've never paid any attention to other commercial rock bands. I've never read a U2 interview so I don't know if there are rumours of them doing insane things. I'm not really aware of any other rock band that has so many rumours written about them. Guns N' Roses went into it admitting stuff, trying to create something, same with Jane's Addiction, who totally flaunted it, totally glamorised heroin use. I think that's ridiculous." KURT, 1992

"I choose to do drugs, but I have nothing good to say about them. They are a total waste of time. We have a lot of young fans, and I don't want anything to do with inciting drug use. People who use drugs are fucked." KURT, 1992

"I knew that when I had a child, I'd be overwhelmed, and it's true. I can't tell you how much my attitude has changed since we've got Frances. Holding my baby is the best drug in the world. I don't want my daughter to grow up with people telling her that her parents were junkies." KURT, 1992

DRUGS & THEIR CONSEQUENCES

"Yeah, I drank. And I was obnoxious when I drank too much. Then there was a period of the last two years of High School when I didn't have any friends, and I didn't drink or do any drugs at all, and I sat in my room and played guitar." **KURT, 1992**

"We did drugs and it was really fun, and now it's over. Anybody who knows me knows I'm way too paranoid to get wasted all the time." COURTNEY, 1992

"He looked like a ghoul. I just figured it's his fucking trip, it's his life, he can do what ever he wants. You can't change anybody or preach some kind of morals or anything. What am I going to do? Nothing. So I just do my own thing." **KRIST NOVOLSELIC ON KURT**

"If you want to ask about my drug problem, go ask my big fat smart ten pound daughter, she'll answer any questions you have about it." COURTNEY, 1992

"Anybody who knows me knows that I'm way too paranoid to get too fucked up. I don't even get that drunk, Y'know? I mean, we did do drugs for a while but it wasn't as mythical or sick as some people make out. It was kinda fun. But then I wanted to have a baby so I stopped. It's that simple." **COURTNEY, 1993**

"I have a responsibility not to promote a negative lifestyle. If I choose to live my life in a negative way which may influence kids to do what I do, then I have no problem telling kids how lame it is to act that way. I never went out of my way to say anything about my drug use. I tried to hide it as long as I could. The main reason was that I didn't want some 15-year old kid who likes our band to think it's cool to do heroin, you know? I think people who glamorise drugs are fucking assholes and, if there is a hell, they'll go there." KURT, 1993

"I've had this terrible stomach problem for years and that has made touring difficult. People would see me sitting in the corner by myself looking sick and gloomy. The reason is that I was trying to fight against the stomach pain, trying to hold my food down. People looked (at) me and assumed I was some kind of addict. I did heroin for three weeks, then I went through a detox program... to straighten myself out again. That took a really long time – about a month." **KURT**

"For five years during the time I had my stomach problem, yeah. I wanted to kill myself every day. I came very close many times. I'm sorry to be so blunt about it. It was to the point where I was on tour, lying on the floor, vomiting air because I couldn't hold down water. And I had to play a show in 20 minutes. I'd sing and cough up blood. This is no way to live a life. I love to play music, but something was not right. So I decided to medicate myself."

KURT, 1994

"I accepted the fact that I was a drug-addict. And I go to the meetings (Narcotics Anonymous)... I am aware I am not above it. I realise that drugs can floor me."

COURTNEY, 1994

"I just decided I wanted to have a life. If I'm going to kill myself, I'm going to kill myself for a reason instead of some stupid stomach problem. So I decided to take everything in excess all at once."

KURT, 1994

"I was determined to get a habit. I wanted to. It was my choice. This is the only thing that's saving me from blowing my head off right now. I've been to ten doctors and nothing they can do about it. I've got to do something to stop this pain. It started with three days in a row of doing heroin and I don't have a stomach pain. That was such a relief. I decided, 'Fuck, I'm going to do this for a whole year. I'll eventually stop. I can't do it forever because I'll fucking die.' I don't regret it at all because it was such a relief from not having stomach pain every day. My mental state just went totally up. I healed myself." KURT, 1994

"I ended up doing a hundred dollar shot in one shot and not even feeling it, hardly. I was just filling up the syringe as far as it would go without pulling the end off. At that point it was like why do it?" KURT ON HIS $400-A-DAY HABIT

"Kurt was very depressed. He tried things like Prozac but opiates were what made him feel better." COURTNEY, 1994

"They were just nodding out in bed, just wasted. It was disgusting and gross. It doesn't make me angry at them, it makes me angry that they would be so pathetic as to do something like that. I think it's pathetic for anyone to do something to make themselves that functionless and a drooling fucking baby. It's like 'Hey, let's do a drug that knocks us out and makes us look stupid'. It's stupid and gross and pathetic for anyone to take it to that point." DAVE GROHL ON KURT AND COURTNEY, 1994

"It was just the times. Everyone was doing it. Everyone in this town (Seattle) did dope. Every-fucking-body. It was unbelievable."
COURTNEY, 1995

"Kurt loved to hang out with dealers. He just thought that was cool. He was really salt-of-the-fucking earth. Kurt Cobain in front of the Jack-in-the-Box, on Broadway, copping a 30-piece. Please. It was just like, 'Kurt, you really have to chill on this shit'." COURTNEY, 1995

DRUGS & THEIR CONSEQUENCES

"Kurt was a gobbler. If you had acid, he'd take acid. If you had mushrooms, he'd take mushrooms. When it came to drugs, he was abusive in a very intense way. If there were 40 pills, he'd take 40 pills, instead of taking two pills and making it last a month. He took eight once, and he got furiously sick. And he refused to take Prozacs ever again because quote, 'They make my stomach hurt', unquote. And I was like, 'Kurt, that's because you took eight of them at one fucking time'." **COURTNEY, 1995**

"The day Frances was born this dealer came to the hospital. There were 8,000 nurses and doctors outside the door, and Kurt was in the hospital, on a morphine drip for his stomach. He's already on a fucking morphine drip, and then he arranges for this dealer to come and stick a needle into the IV. And he like totally died. He would totally die all the time. Some people OD. I've never OD'ed, ever. I've gotten real fucking blasto, but instead of ODing, I chatter and start talking too much, screaming and running around naked and getting hysterical, cutting my arms, you know crazy shit. Breaking windows. But I have never fallen on the floor blue." COURTNEY, 1995

"In hospital he almost died. The dealer said she'd never seen someone so dead. I said, 'Why didn't you get a nurse? There are nurses all over the place'." **COURTNEY, 1994**

"The day of the New York show at Roseland (July 23, 1993) Kurt totally died. His eyes were wide-fucking-open, like a cadaver. Dead. It was awful. I made Wendy come up one time, and I'm like, 'This is your fucking son', and just threw him at her. And he was right over there, and he just looked at her and said (in a junkies croak): 'I'm not on drugs, Mom. I'm not on drugs. Uhhhh'. And after Rome I completely lost influence with him." COURTNEY

"You can't be around rock'n'roll and a husband on drugs and stuff without it getting to you. But I do not want to go down that road. Memories hurt too much." **COURTNEY, 1997**

DRUGS & THEIR CONSEQUENCES

Kurt's March 3 Suicide Attempt

"Kurt had gone on out for me when I got there (Rome). He'd gotten me roses. He'd gotten me a piece of the Coliseum, because he knows that I love Roman History. I had some champagne, took a valium, we made out, I fell asleep. The rejection he must have felt after all that anticipation... I mean, for Kurt to be that Mr. Romance was pretty intense. I turned over about three or four in the morning to make love, and he was gone. He was at the end of the bed with a thousand dollars in his pocket and a note saying, 'You don't love me anymore. I'd rather die than go through a divorce'. It was all in his head. I'd been away from him during our relationship maybe 60 days. I had to do my thing. I can see how it happened. He took 50 fucking pills. He probably forgot how many he took. But there was a definite suicidal urge to be gobbling and gobbling. Goddamn, man. Even if I wasn't in the mood. I should have just laid there for him. All he needed was to get laid. He would have been fine. But with Kurt you had to give yourself to him. He was psychic. He could tell if you were not all the way there. Sex, to him was incredibly sacred. He found commitment to be an aphrodisiac. Yeah, he definitely left a note in the room. I was told to shut-up about it. And what could the media have done to help him." COURTNEY, 1994

"I hadn't seen him for 26 days, which was the longest we'd gone without seeing each other since we'd been together. He was nervous, too. He knew how obsessed I am with Roman history, and he got this beautiful hotel room and he covered it with flowers. He went to the Coliseum and he kicked a rock off. Man, I haven't touched these since. And these are rosaries from the Vatican that he bought me. And he bought me these beautiful jewels, some three carat diamonds earrings, and some roses. Which I thought was beautiful. It was not his deal. He was not Mr. Romance. He even bought me lingerie. And so we ordered champagne, 'cause Pat Smear was with us for a little while, and Kurt doesn't drink, and then we put Frances to bed. And we started making out, and we fell asleep. He must have woken up and started writing a letter about how he felt rejected. But I'm not sure I believe that because he wasn't rejected. We both fell asleep. Anyway, I woke up at, like, four in the morning to reach for him, basically to go fuck him, 'cause I hadn't seen him in so long. And he wasn't there. And I always get alarmed when Kurt's not there, 'cause I figure he's in the corner somewhere, doing something bad. And he's on the floor, and he's dead. There's blood coming out of his nostril. And he's fully dressed. He's in a corduroy coat, and he's got 1,000 American dollars clutched in one hand, which was grey, and a note in the other. It was on hotel stationary, and he was talking about how I'm not in love with him anymore, and he can't go through another divorce (referring to his parents). And then the next page is like how we're destined to be together, and how he knows how much I love him, and please don't take this personally. **"** COURTNEY, 1995

"I just held his ass. I just held him. I felt like I really needed to show him that I loved him, and you know, 'please stop this'. I may seem quite flip and everything now, but I was not flip then. I was catatonic. I really was over the edge. And there was a third person involved here. It just wasn't between me and Kurt. It was me and Kurt and Frances. **" COURTNEY, 1995**

DRUGS & **THEIR CONSEQUENCES**

On The Road

"NIRVANA: FUDGE PACKING, CRACK SMOKING, SATAN WORSHIPING MOTHERFUCKERS.**"** **SLOGAN ON THE BACK OF NIRVANA TOUR T-SHIRT**

"We're not gonna' be proud of the fact there are a bunch of Guns N' Roses kids who are into our music. We don't feel comfortable progressing, playing larger venues." KURT, 1991

"It's a nice feeling, it needs to be done at least twice a week. It seems to be becoming more common at our gigs. The more people are screaming at you, the more you are into smashing everything up. It's definitely not a contrived thing. We don't smash the gear up on purpose, we're not trying to impress or anything.**"**
KRIST NOLOSELIC ON NIRVANA'S INFAMOUS RITUAL OF DESTROYING ALL THEIR EQUIPMENT AT THE END OF A SHOW

"Just to survive lately, I've become a lot more withdrawn from the band. I don't go party after the show, I go straight to the hotel room and go to sleep and concentrate on eating in the morning. I'd rather deal with things like that. Our friendship isn't being jeopardised by it, but this tour has definitely taken some years off our lives. I plan to make changes." KURT, 1992

"Why are they screaming? What do they see in us? They're exactly the same kind of people who wanted to kick our ass in High School. It's just boring to play outdoors. I've only gotten' used to playing larger venues because the sound is at least tolerable. But, outside, the wind blows the music around so much that it doesn't feel like you're playing music, it feels like you're lip-synching to a boom box recording. Plus, these festivals are very mainstream – we're playing with Extreme and Pearl Jam, you know. Ninety per cent of the kids out there are probably just as much into Extreme as they are into us.**"** **KURT, 1992**

"I don't think pretending to be a professional rock unit really works. If we're gonna' have a shitty show, let's have a shitty show." KURT, 1992

"I don't nearly do it as much as everyone thinks I do. I just wait for a good time to do it – like when I'm pissed off, or if I want to show off in front of Courtney.**"** **KURT COBAIN ON DESTROYING INSTRUMENTS ON STAGE, 1992**

"Last year's shows were way better. I don't think we've had a long enough break. I'm not enjoying it as much as I should. According to our manager and most of the people we work with, the break that we had was too long. Everyone wants us to work and work all the time, and not stop. It was only four months of relaxation and I really needed that. I've come to a lot of conclusions about myself within the last four months. I've learned to accept the fact of being a rock star and how big the band's become. I can at least deal with it, I'm not as pissed off as I was. It's still... I dunno. I'm such a picky person that everything has to be perfect." KURT, 1992

"I don't even remember the guitar solo on 'Teen Spirit'. It would take me five minutes to sit in the catering room and learn the solo. But I'm not interested in that stuff. I don't know, if that's so lazy that I don't care anymore or what. I still like playing 'Teen Spirit', but it's almost an embarrassment to play it.**"** **KURT, 1994**

ON THE ROAD

"I don't want to use this as an excuse, and it's come up so many times, but my stomach ailment has been one of the biggest barriers that stopped us from touring. I was dealing with it for a long time. But after a person experiences chronic pain for five years, by the time that fifty year ends, you're literally insane. I couldn't cope with anything, I was as schizophrenic as a wet cat that's been beaten.**"** KURT, 1994

"For a few years in Seattle, it was the Summer Of Love, and it was so great. To be able to jump out on top of the crowd with my guitar and be held up and pushed to the back of the room, and then brought back with no harm done to me... it was a celebration of something no-one could put their finger on. But once it got into the mainstream, it was over. I'm just tired of being embarrassed by it. I'm beyond that.**"** **KURT, 1994**

Politics: Corporate or Otherwise

"VANDALISM: BEAUTIFUL AS A ROCK IN A COP'S FACE.**"**

STICKER ON THE SIDE OF ONE OF KURT'S GUITARS

"A big factor (in creating *Nevermind*) has been a lot of political and social discontent. When we went to make this record, I had such a feeling of us vs. them. All those people waving the flag and being brainwashed, I really hated them. And all of a sudden, they're all buying our record, and I just think, 'You don't get it at all'." KRIST NOVOSELIC, 1992

"You know what I hate about rock? Cartoons and horns. I hate Phil Collins, all of that white male soul. I hate tied-dyed tee-shirts of Nirvana. I hate that. I wouldn't wear a tied-dyed tee-shirt unless it was dyed with the urine of Phil Collins and the blood of Jerry Garcia.**"** **KURT, 1992**

**"I don't see how people can get the idea that I'm stupid, because I know my music's semi-intelligent. I know it takes a bit of creativity to write the kind of music I do, it's not just a wall of noise. I know there's a formula to it, and I've worked really hard at it. I've always been the kind of person that if I think someone thinks of me a certain way – like I'm stupid – then I'll act stupid in front of them. I've never felt the need to prove myself.
If someone already has a misconception about me, then fine, let them have it all the more. I'll be happy to massage that."**

KURT, 1992

KURT & **COURTNEY** *Talking*

Q: **"**You seem to complain
about the empathy of our
generation, is that right?**"**
A: **"**Whatever you want to
make out of it, it's up to
you.... it's your crossword
puzzle.**"** KURT, 1992

**"It's impossible to be
subversive in the
commercial world
because they'll crucify
you for it. You can't get
away with it. We've
tried, and we've been
almost ruined by it."**
KURT, 1992

"I'm more attuned to class than I've ever
been, and the record company here literally treats us like shit.**"**
COURTNEY, 1998

**"Somebody wrote 'How can she rock in a Versace gown?'
Well, easy, let me show you."** COURTNEY, 1997

"As a celebrity my name gets attached to trash all the time but
I do it on purpose. Look, I did a Versace campaign and I HAD FUN!
But it wasn't creative output. Creative output is a different deal
and I take it pretty seriously.**"** COURTNEY, 1999

**"I threw a real fit at a recent awards show. They gave my band,
Hole, just meat and cheese to eat and wouldn't allow us time to
rehearse for our spot. Now, if you've been to upper-class schools
or you're an actress like Gwyneth Paltrow, you get treated well.
But us rock kids are considered to be uneducated, so the attitude
is to treat us like crap."** COURTNEY, 1999

66 Eddie Vedder was right. When he took on Ticketmaster, nobody stood up with this guy. That image of him standing up alone in front of Congress has haunted me. And by the way, where were U2 and R.E.M. and everyone else at that moment? 99 **COURTNEY, 2001**

Retaining a Punk Ethic Vs Fame & Success in The Corporate World...

66 People want me to be evil because of how I come across on stage and on record. People really, really do want me to be evil... and I'm really kind of not. 99 **COURTNEY, 1991**

66 **I went to lunch with this corporate weasel the other day, and he just said, 'What do you want to do?', and I said I wanted to go see Nirvana in Chicago, so he gave me a thousand dollars.** 99 COURTNEY, 1991

66 We (Hole) do have corporate interest, but were just not ready. For a band with our ideology, the only reason to have a corporate label is for better distribution. So if we sell enough records that we need that, then I'll think about it. 99

COURTNEY, 1991

POLITICS

"We (Nirvana) weren't prepared for it (fame), it's never been a main goal of ours, we don't care about anything like that we just wanted to put out a record, the people that liked our first album will like this one also. Of course we wanted to make a comfortable living at it, at least to eat, to travel and tour but as far as getting in the Top 10 we didn't care at all, we knew it wouldn't last for very long." KURT, 1992

"It's not a matter of destroying the music industry, it's a question of being able to be included. Egalitarian revolution – that's what makes them a punk-rock band."

JONATHAN PONEMAN, CO-OWNER OF SUB-POP, ON NIRVANA

"This really insane, weird thing happened with her. I think she wanted to buy not only us but all these underground bands she doesn't have a clue about, like Pavement and Cell. I pretty much only had one in-depth conversation with her, and she was going on about being a revolutionary. I'd sold like two records compared to her, and I didn't feel competitive or anything, but I felt like I'd hate her to be the person who put our records out. When you fuck with Jesus or God or whoever she thinks she is, you pay a price." COURTNEY ON MADONNA AND HER MAVERICK LABEL

"I wish I had never come in to her (Madonna's) eye-line. Isn't there any punk rock value in the fact that I turned her down and then she sent over one of her toadies to execute me? The *Vanity Fair* piece would never have happened if I hadn't turned her down."

COURTNEY, BLAMING MADONNA AND HER MAVERICK LABEL FOR THE
DAMAGING *VANITY FAIR* ARTICLE

"I have this weird sense of liberation now. Did it take money to liberate me, or was it just that I got older? I'm not going to bust my ass for The Man ever again, that's for sure. Even if I'm broke, I'm not going to return to that mainstream culture. I'll join a commune, go get a thatched hut in the woods."

KRIST NOVOSELIC, 1992

“ We (Nirvana) were the chosen rejects, we chose not to be a part of the popular crowd. I can remember a lot of times, the more popular people, the jock type kind of people who were into sports and staying clean and brushing their teeth all the time and doing what their parents were asking them to do. They always asked me if I wanted to join their little clubs... I would rather be with the people who didn't... and who would smoke cigarettes and would listen to rock'n'roll instead. ” **KURT, 1992**

“ **We wanted to do as good as Sonic Youth. We thought we'd sell a couple of hundred thousand records at the most, and that would be fine. Next thing you know, we go Top 10. I wish we could have a time machine and go back to two months ago. I'd tell people to get lost.** ” KRIST NOVOSELIC, 1992

“ I knew we (Nirvana) were going to be popular, but I didn't know we were going to be this popular. I'm so tired of saying this. I'm so tired of saying, 'Oh, we thought we were going to be as big as Sonic Youth', and all that shit. It's so fucking boring at this point. ”

KURT, 1993

“ **I think of myself as a success because I still haven't compromised my music, but that's just speaking on an artistic level. Obviously, all the other parts that belong with success are just driving me insane. What I really can't stand about being successful is when people confront me and say, 'Oh, you should just mellow out and enjoy it'. I don't know how many times I have to fucking say this.** *I never wanted it in the first place.* ” KURT, 1993

> "I was always more of a feminine person when I was young."

'The boys can take off their shirts when they get hot, so why can't I?"

,,

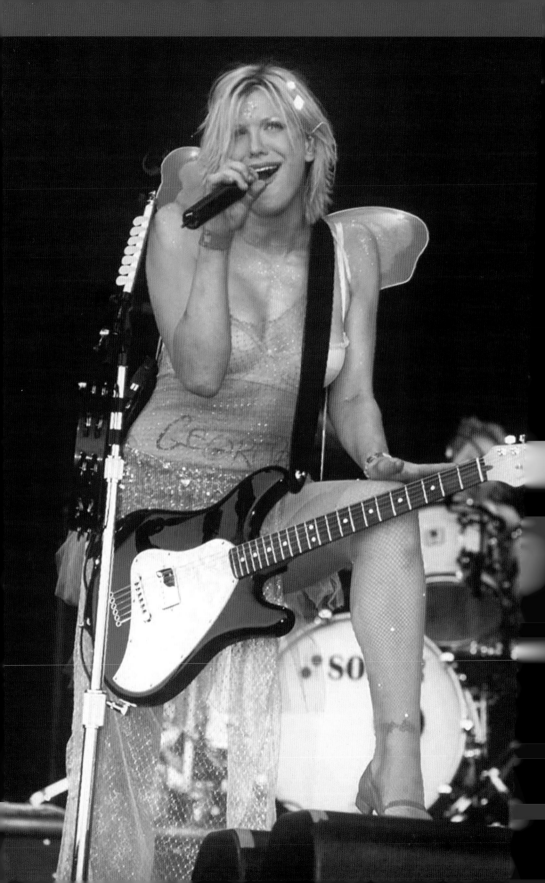

"It's like Evian water and battery acid. And when you mix the two you get love."

"I've got the same tastes as fags, I'm a total drag-queen fag."

" I do enjoy the money. It's at least a sense of security. I know that my child's going to grow up and be able to eat. That's a really nice feeling. **"** KURT, 1993

" People say Kurt's destroyed punk rock... And me and L7 and Helmet, we signed to majors, we destroyed it too. Just because I signed to a major label doesn't make me into Madonna or Wendy James, y'know? **"**

COURTNEY, 1993

" I got Axl Rose so furious he tried to punch me. I mean, to me, that was it. It wasn't much but I did my part. When me and Kurt were leaving the MTV awards Kurt said, 'We have Axl, Madonna and Michael Jackson mad at us. We should hide, that's worse than the FBI!' **"** COURTNEY, 1993

" A few years ago, we were in Detroit, playing at this club, and about ten people showed up. And next door, there was this bar, and Axl Rose came in with ten or fifteen bodyguards. It was this huge extravaganza; all these people fawning over him. If he'd just walked in by himself it would have been no big deal. But he wanted that. You create attention to attract attention. **"** KURT, 1994

" It was so fast and explosive. I didn't know how to deal with it. If there was a Rock Star 101 course, I would have liked to take it. It might have helped me. **"** KURT, 1994

POLITICS

"I've found myself doing the same things that a lot of other rock stars do or are forced to do. Which is not being able to respond to mail, not being able to keep up on current music, and I'm pretty much locked away a lot. The outside world is pretty foreign to me." KURT, 1994

"I just got a cheque a while ago for some royalties for *Nevermind*, which is a pretty good size. It's weird, though, really weird. When we were selling a lot of records during *Nevermind*, I thought, 'God I'm gonna' have like $10 million, $15 million'. But that's not the case. We do not live large. I still eat Kraft macaroni and cheese – because I like it, I'm used to it. We're not extravagent people. I don't blame any kid for thinking that a person who sells 10 million records is a millionaire and is set for the rest of his life. But it's not the case. I spent a million dollars last year, and I have no idea how I did it. Really, I bought a house for $400,000. Taxes were another £300,00 – or something. What else? I lent my mom some money. I bought a car. That was about it." **KURT, 1994**

"Years ago in a certain town, my reputation had gotten so bad that every time I went to a party, I was expected to burn the place down and knock out every window. So I would go into social situations and try my best to be really graceful and quiet and aloof. But sometimes when people are bearing down on you so hard, and want you to behave in a certain way you just do it because you know you can. I'm so busy these day pleading with everyone that I'm lucid, that I'm educated, that I'm middle-class. It's stupid. If you ask me, why aren't people on the cases of the real assholes of this world, like Axl Rose and Steve Albini, both of whom should be exterminated. Really, they should leave on a shuttle to the sun. The shouldn't be on the earth. Because they're not good for anything." COURTNEY, 1994

Kurt & Courtney's Rivalry

❝I'm driven. I am. I'm driven, for some reason. But I don't know where I'm going.❞ **COURTNEY, 1991**

❝So Kurt and I get married and we're peers – his band were always ahead, but they started before us – then, suddenly his band get real successful and we're not peers anymore. He's involved in free trade in America and I'm not making much of a dent. It's just really amazing to see.❞ COURTNEY, 1992

❝The attitude is that Kurt's more important than me, because he sells more records. Well, fuck you! Suck my dick!❞ **COURTNEY, 1993**

❝When I married Kurt, there were a lot of women, who rather than thinking, 'I'm gonna' be the man I want to marry, I'm going to be the best rock star, I'm going to get the man I wanna' marry'. That, to me, is culturally deplorable. It's one of the few things I am completely crystal clear about. Y'know, I never in my life thought that I would live off someone else's money. Nothing that I've ever done has indicated that I've had anything other than loser boyfriends that live off me so it's a very pleasant surprise that I get to live in a nice house and can afford to have a baby. That's great and I'm pleased with it but I don't want to spend Kurt's money. I mean in one breath people say I got a million dollars from Geffen and in the next they say I'm a gold digger. I mean, a million's not enough? Maybe people are jealous, I don't know.❞

COURTNEY, 1993

KURT & **COURTNEY** *Talking*

" The only time I asked him for a riff for one of my songs, he was in the closet. We had this huge closet, and I heard him in there working on 'Heart Shaped Box'. He did that in five minutes. Knock, Knock, Knock. 'What?' 'Do you need that riff?' 'Fuck you!' "

COURTNEY, 1994

" **Even if I was talentless... after seeing Echo & The Bunnymen eight million times and Nirvana ten million times, how could I not write an OK new wave record?** " COURTNEY, 1995

" I think that I'm competitive in an American, good way. I don't think I'm competitive in a shitty way. I'm not a bad sport; I want to respect my enemy. You know, when we toured with Mudhoney, I would walk into their dressing room every night: 'Jerks, Punks, are you ready? 'Cause I'm going to kick your ass'. I've always been that way, and it inspires me. It's what makes me go. Not insurmountable odds, but interesting, fun stuff. Like, 'God, if she can do it or he can do it, I can do it too!' All The Pixies' records were amazing to me, so I felt very competitive in terms of the way Kim Deal and Charles(Thompson) wrote songs. And the way that Kurt wrote songs. Back when Kurt was just, like, a guy that I thought was a bit of a dick, I heard 'In Bloom' in my publicist's office, and it really woke me up. I find his song writing to be impeccable. " **COURTNEY**

" **Kathleen Hanna was my husband's worst enemy in the world; someone who would stop at nothing to aggravate us. Funny that they refer to her as being in a band. She's not really in a band. Bikini Kill don't really play and they don't really write songs. She's a political activist who took a bunch of women's studies classes.** " COURTNEY, 1994

Frances Bean Cobain

"They filed a legal report on me based on *Vanity Fair* and nothing else, no other fucking evidence, that I was an unfit mother. That I smoked during my pregnancy. Fuck you, everybody smokes during their pregnancy – who gives a shit? And it's because I married Kurt, because he's hot, young and cute." COURTNEY, 1992

"Having a wife and child can obviously change your perspective on things. Like, two years ago I never thought about the future, not at all. But now I have this huge responsibility to my family and it's probably more pressure than I've every had dealing with this band. Now I'm thinking about not leaving the child in the car, not even for a second, in case someone snatches her, all kinds of things like that.In the last year and a half even before we found out Courtney was pregnant, I've started to evolve a little bit from being a

KURT & **COURTNEY** *Talking*

completely negative bastard, pretending to be punk rock and hating the world, and saying clichéd things like, 'Anyone who brings a child in to the world at this point is completely selfish'. KURT, 1993

There's some sort of mother blood that just wants you to buy firearms when you have a child. She's like this perfection, this innocence, this utter and total purity that's uncorrupted by anything. And if somebody was to hurt or deride or in any way fuck with my child I would not hesitate to kill them. **COURTNEY, 1993**

She seems to be attracted to almost anyone. She loves anyone. And it saddens me to know that she's moved around so much. We do have two nannies, one full-time and another older woman who takes care of her on weekends. But when we take her on the road, she's around people all the time, and she doesn't get to go to the park very often. We try as hard as we can, we take her to pre-school things. But this is a totally different world. KURT, 1994

Even if Courtney and I were to get divorced, I would never allow us to be in a situation where there are bad vibes between us in front of her. That kind of stuff can screw up a kid, but the reason that those things happen is because the parents are not very bright.

KURT, 1994

I don't think that Courtney and I are that fucked-up. We have lacked love all our lives, and we need it so much that if there's any goal that we have, it's to give Frances as much love as we can. That's the one thing that I know is not going to turn out bad. KURT, 1994

People are gonna make fun of her, make fun of her dad, and she's gonna feel like she's not good enough for him, and she'll probably feel ugly. He thought he was doing the right thing (suicide). How could he fucking think that? In this condition he was so fucked up to think that. If I could have just spoken two words to him...

And then he would have OD'd when he was about 34 or 35. But at least he would have had those seven years to make his decision to be a heroin addict forever. Or whatever the hell it is he wanted. **"**

COURTNEY, 1994

"I don't care if people think I'm exploiting my child. She's the only successful thing I've done in my life." COURTNEY, 1995

"I have a big mouth, and I talk about a lot of stuff. But I've always found it hard to discuss my child. Because she's *my* child, and it's private. So fuck you. I don't think I'm going to do it anymore (talk about Frances in interviews), because it's getting to the point where her face is recognisable, and I'm worried about some crazy asshole kidnapping her.**"** **COURTNEY, 1995**

"My greatest excitement these days is to spend a quiet evening at home with my daughter Frances, or we might go horse riding in Malibu. I'm beginning to behave in a grown-up way."

COURTNEY, 1999

FRANCES BEAN COBAIN

Feminism & Riot Grrrl

"Being aware of not offending women and of not supporting sexist acts. But not so you become so paranoid that you can't feel comfortable in a woman's presence. Sexist jokes are harmless as long as you are aware of them, but I also know a lot of people who put on this pretend macho redneck act twenty four hours a day – they use the red neck lingo and spew out sexist quotes – again and then they claim that they're simply trying to remind you that's how rednecks are. I've noticed that if someone does that for too long they become a redneck." **KURT, 1992**

"**It means women controlling their own lives, and me not standing in their way by being a male. It's not so much of an ideal as a sense. It doesn't seem like there's such a thing as a recognisable feminist movement like there was during the Seventies, more a collective awareness. It's in the way you live your life.**" KURT, 1992

"They're mostly strippers, they all have flat stomachs and they wear hip-huggers. They write their own fanzines, which are kind of like SCUM manifestos for 12-year-olds. It's all about girl love – don't let boys destroy our love for each other – it's about girls, not women. It's threatening in its cuteness. But some of them are older than me they're like 28, 29." **COURTNEY, 1992**

"**There's a song on the album about Frances Farmer getting her revenge on Seattle. Kurt believes that when Mount St Helens erupts again it will be Frances getting her own back on the city. The song is so feminine. Men don't often write poetry equating women with nature.**" COURTNEY, 1993

KURT & **COURTNEY** *Talking*

"People hate her, they really do. Did you know that to 'Yoko' someone is a verb in America? It's something that boys say if they're hanging out with you too much and they're going to school or they have a band. It's almost a myth that's used to suppress women. Y'know, 'You're gonna Yoko me. You're gonna' destroy me'. And this woman put up with racial inequality from Fleet Street, she put up with being accused of breaking up the best band in the world, she put up with people's idea that she castrated this man and then, worst of all, she had her best friend, her husband, the person she lived for, die in her arms in front of a fortress that she'd hidden herself in for 20 years. And I just feel that the world media should apologise to her because she handled it with so much dignity. I don't think she's ever even done anything defensive. She's never done interviews, like me, like, 'I DID NOT FUCK YOU!' She always just kept her mouth shut."

COURTNEY ON YOKO ONO, 1993

"Y'know, hairy, maternal, it menstruates, it's a mother, it's ugly. I think the reason the media is so excited about it is because its saying females are inept, females are naive, females are innocent, clumsy, bratty..." COURTNEY ON RIOT GRRRL

"I tried to start a Riot Grrrl chapter in LA at one point. I called a bunch of people to try to set up a meeting, and they were like, 'But the place will be bugged! *A Current Affair* will be there! And I'm like, 'Listen, nobody cares, girls. Interest is on the wane in this little fad'." **COURTNEY, 1994**

"There will always be physical differences between men and women that I respect and love, which is why I'm a hetrosexual, thank you very much. The problem with rock is testosterone is getting kicked out of it, and part of rock is dick, part of rock is going to see a gig and wanting to fuck the guy. I didn't get into this to chop off everyone's dick and have nothing but girls playing music. That's ridiculous." COURTNEY, 1995

"In this female genre, we've (Hole) sold more than anyone. We've sold more than the metal boys. But it bugs me. I like there to be some testosterone in rock and it's like, I'm the one in the dress who has to provide it! These wimpy fucking boys, Pavement, sitting there whining about something. That's what Jane's Addiction had that was good – muscle, metal. And we have too; we have some really good metal songs.**" COURTNEY, 1995**

"Girl power? It's just a con, hatched by a bunch of businessmen to sell to young girls, to rob them of the slogan for real so they can never, ever, use it for what it purports to stand for. It's like the business world's revenge on riot grrrl; they've flogged it like soap powder..." COURTNEY ON THE SPICE GIRLS, 1998

"I've been in so many rehearsal studios where someone starts playing a hook and somebody else goes, 'It's too cheesy! It's too cheesy!' And it's fine to be on that side of the fence. Go! Go! Go! Go be Ian MacKaye, go be that. But the truth is, they have trust funds or else they really believe it and they end up... banquet-hall hostesses because they can't be strippers any more because now they're too old.**" COURTNEY, 1998**

"I just did a show in Danford, Connecticut where, for the first time in my life, they weren't 15-year-old girls, they were eight! And nine! And ten! And eleven! It wasn't that I didn't like them, but they were these tiny little girls with their dads at the back and I didn't know how to embrace it." COURTNEY, 1999

"The boys can take of their shirts when they get hot, so why can't I?**"** COURTNEY, 1999

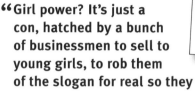

FEMINISM & RIOT GRRRL

"The boys get all weird when you sell as many or more than they do. It's rare for a female who plays rock so they really want a piece of you one way or another – a piece of your ass, a piece of your history, a piece of immortality – by being one of your 'helpers'. They wanna fuck you, and if you spend one night in a room they scream they wrote everything or (in the most recent case) they simply beg you to help them sell tickets and pull the plug when you're at your most vulnerable. I'm used to it, and I'm very flattered. I just wish I had a bigger sorority." COURTNEY, 2001

"I'm sorry to say, but the last fully-formed, all-female band that was serious and meant a damned thing in terms of musicianship was The Bangles. I say this with all affection for the girls I started out with – and obviously I adore and respect The Breeders, PJ Harvey and Lucinda Williams – but these are singular women, not a band working together. There is in every band a leader, and that's important." **COURTNEY, 2001**

"I love her (Kelly Osbourne's) song 'Shut The Fuck Up'. She's got the real thing in her. I had her for three days and it was fun. She really does have something going on."
COURTNEY, 2003

"It's time for Eminem to go. He's a fucking sexist. He's not good for my fucking daughter. I want a good world for my daughter. When I saw 'It's so boring without me' in that song ('Without Me'), I just figured he'd written a nice song about me!"
COURTNEY, 2003

Fans &
True Fans

❝I don't blame the average 17-year old punk-rock kid for calling me a sell-out. I understand that. Maybe when they grow up a bit, they'll realise there's more things to life than living out your rock and roll identity so righteously.❞ **KURT, 1992**

❝**Metal's searching for an identity because it's exhausted itself, so they're going to latch onto us. We're not metal fans. There's a lack of insight into anything on a higher level. A lot of heavy metal kids are just plain dumb. I'm sorry. We're heavy, but we're not heavy metal.**❞ KRIST NOVOSELIC, 1992

❝You know, a person can say a lot of stupid things when they're going through stressful times in their life. I don't regret the majority of things I was trying to convey, but they didn't really translate right. And there was a handful of things I can remember that I really do regret us saying. Like when Chris said, 'For the most part, heavy metal kids are just stupid'. I couldn't say that. I was a heavy metal kid at one time. That's just way too insulting, it's too extreme a thing to say. You have to elaborate on things like that, or not say them at all.❞ **KURT, 1992**

❝**Well it's a bit embarrassing to play in front of kids who wear Skid Row T-shirts, y'know? It's really hard to overcome that, to just shake it off and say, 'Oh well, they're just dumb kids, maybe they'll throw away their Skid Row records and listen to Mudhoney because of us...' but that story's old. I'm tired of talking about the underground! I've never claimed to be a punk rocker, I've just claimed to have liked punk rock**

KURT & **COURTNEY** *Talking*

music. I'd like to be a rhythm guitar player in a band! No one realises how fucking hard it is to scream at the top of your lungs and concentrate on playing guitar solos. KURT, 1992

"I can't have a lot of animosity toward them (middle-of-the-road rock-jock fans), because a lot of people's personalities aren't necessarily their choice – a lot of times, they're pushed into the way they live. Hopefully, they'll like our music and listen to something else that's in the same vein, that's a bit different from Van Halen. Hopefully they will be exposed to the underground by reading interviews with us. Knowing that we do come from a punk-rock world, maybe they'll look into that and change their ways a bit.**" KURT, 1992**

"We played in Atlanta on Halloween, and all these weird purists showed up. Total fans, but every time we'd go into one of our pop songs, they'd start chanting: 'Don't do it! Sellout!' I heard one girl saying to this other girl, 'They used to be so much better'. So I just started talking to the audience. I said, 'I've grown, you haven't, the sex really isn't good anymore, and you know what? There's always going to be a shitty band with girls in it that can't play'. Girls were throwing Riot Grrrl 'zines at me and stuff. I was like, 'Uh, I'm really glad you're here, girls, but check it out: I can write a bridge now'." COURTNEY, 1993

"I definitely have a problem with the average macho-man, the strong-oxen working class type, because they have always been a threat to me. I've had to deal with them most of my life – being taunted and beaten up by them in school, just having to be around them and be expected to be that kind of person when you grow up. I definitely feel closer to the feminine side of the human being than I do the male – or the American idea of what a male is supposed to be. Just watch a beer commercial, and you'll see what I mean.**"

KURT

"I don't have as many judgements about them as I used to. I've come to terms about why they're there and we're here. It doesn't bother me anymore to see this Neanderthal with a moustache, out of his mind, drunk, singing along to 'Sliver'." KURT, 1994

Bi, Hetro & Ex's

❝I didn't find any of the girls in my high school attractive. They had really awful haircuts and fucked-up attitudes. So I thought I would try to be gay for a while.**❞ KURT, 1991**

❝I started being proud of the fact that I was gay even though I wasn't. I really liked the conflict. It was pretty exciting. I was a special geek. I wasn't quite the punk rocker I was looking for, but at least it was better than being the average geek.❞ KURT

❝I've had the reputation of being a homosexual ever since I was 14. It was really cool because I found a couple of gay friends in Aberdeen – which was almost impossible. I got beat up a lot, of course, because of my association with them. People just thought I was weird, at first, just some fucked-up kid. But once I got the gay tag, it gave me the freedom to be able to be a freak and let people know they should stay away from me. It made for quite a few scary experiences in alleys walking home from school, too.**❞ KURT, 1991**

❝I'm definitely gay in spirit, and I probably could be bisexual. If I wouldn't have found Courtney, I probably would have carried on a bisexual lifestyle.❞ KURT, 1993

❝Well, can I say first there's no such things as bisexuality, no such fucking thing. You definitely have a preference – everyone has a preference. I've had a lot of sex, a lot, and I've fucked up, I dunno, 14 girls? Fifteen? But when it comes down to it I just want someone to stick it in, y'know?**❞ KURT, 1994**

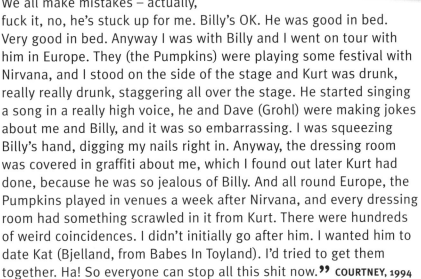

❝I lost my virginity in a council house in Liverpool, listening to 'Isolation' by Joy Division, to a guy called Michael Mooney, who hung around with The Teardrop Explodes. After we'd done it I went across the road for cigarettes and I had all this blood and fluids running down my legs. Luuurgh, real graphic.❞

COURTNEY, 1994

❝I was going out with Billy Corgan (The Smashing Pumpkins) for my sins. We all make mistakes – actually, fuck it, no, he's stuck up for me. Billy's OK. He was good in bed. Very good in bed. Anyway I was with Billy and I went on tour with him in Europe. They (the Pumpkins) were playing some festival with Nirvana, and I stood on the side of the stage and Kurt was drunk, really really drunk, staggering all over the stage. He started singing a song in a really high voice, he and Dave (Grohl) were making jokes about me and Billy, and it was so embarrassing. I was squeezing Billy's hand, digging my nails right in. Anyway, the dressing room was covered in graffiti about me, which I found out later Kurt had done, because he was so jealous of Billy. And all round Europe, the Pumpkins played in venues a week after Nirvana, and every dressing room had something scrawled in it from Kurt. There were hundreds of weird coincidences. I didn't initially go after him. I wanted him to date Kat (Bjelland, from Babes In Toyland). I'd tried to get them together. Ha! So everyone can stop all this shit now.❞ COURTNEY, 1994

❝Everyone thinks Evan (Dando) and I are fucking. Evan only fucks 15-year olds!❞ COURTNEY, LIVE ON STAGE IN SYDNEY, REFUTING SPECULATION THAT SHE WAS ROMANTICALLY INVOLVED WITH THE LEMONHEADS SINGER EVAN DANDO, 1995

BI, HETRO & EX'S

❝My relationship with Trent was a minor or major disaster, depending on your perspective. I really liked him a lot as a friend, and I was surprised to find out we had so much in common. What angers me the most, though, is that I think at one point he probably sat down and said, 'What does this do for my image?' He is that image-oriented, even though I pretended that element did not even exist. I was in full denial. I thought he would have a lot of problems like Kurt, but that I could fix them. Like his silver Porsche, like having to prove to himself that he's a rock-star. I thought that these were erratic little problems and I could smooth them over, and make him perfect. Because he really does have a large IQ and he really is sensitive. And I can't think of another male except for my husband who writes lyrics in such a feminine, graphic way. I saw a lot of cool things in Trent, but I was also projecting a lot of Kurt onto him. The whole thing was just too soon after Kurt, ultimately, and I really regret it.❞ COURTNEY ON
HER RELATIONSHIP WITH NINE INCH NAILS FRONTMAN TRENT REZNOR, 1995

❝My friendship with Michael is really complicated and strange. I'm halfway in love with him. Kurt was halfway in love with him. Together, we were sort of love with him in this sort of nonsexual, romantic, and worshipful way... Michael's been absolutely supportive of me (after Kurt's death). He's really been my friend. His perception of me, though, is pretty distorted; he loves me, but he believes a lot of the hyperbole about me, and that really gets to me. I know he has a great respect for my music, but he thinks I love the drama and the starmaking bullshit a lot more than I do.❞
COURTNEY ON HER RELATIONSHIP
WITH R.E.M.'S MICHAEL STIPE, 1995

COURTNEY WITH MICHAEL STIPE

"Mary Lou Lord once gave Kurt a blow job and has built her career on it. There are five people in the world that if I ever run into I will fucking kill, and she is definitely one of them.' **COURTNEY ON ONE OF KURT'S UNLUCKY EX'S, 1995**

"My standard of what a loser is is pretty high. He must have a soaring IQ and be pretty twisted." COURTNEY, 1995

"I've got the same tastes as fags, I go for the rough trade boys. I'm a total drag-queen fag." **COURTNEY, 1995**

WITH JIM BARBER

"It's kinda weird when someone denies knowing you intimately, and two men have done it in the course of 18 months. Like excuse me, am I the gross one? Is it because I'm repulsive? Is it because I'm a widow? Do they want to go where Kurt's been?"

COURTNEY ON MICHAEL MOONEY AND TRENT REZNOR WHO BOTH PUBLICLY REFUSE TO ACKNOWLEDGE THEIR RELATIONSHIP WITH HER, 1995

"I really have this secret obsession with him (Michael Douglas), which I just can't get rid of." **COURTNEY, 1997**

"Russell (Crowe) is a really interesting and dark guy. Even just holding his hand I get shivers. He goes through hell. But I don't know if he's seen as many dead bodies as I have." COURTNEY, 2003

WITH JIM CAREY

BI, HETRO & EX'S

Media, Privacy & Good Behaviour

❝I thought, if I was in *Vanity Fair*, it would shut their fucking mouths and they'd leave me in peace. But that was my mistake and I just shouldn't have done it. I should have known more about the mainstream press and how they operate.**❞**

COURTNEY ON THE DAMAGING *VANITY FAIR* ARTICLE, 1992

❝I don't know how to explain what happens to me when I do an interview, because I usually shut myself off. It's really hard to explain. I just don't like to get intimate. I don't want anyone to know what I feel and what I think, and if they can't get some sort of idea of what sort of person I am through my music, then that's too bad.❞ KURT, 1992

❝You can't please everybody. I don't care if I get criticised. I don't give a shit if I get a bad review. I don't care if people say I'm a bitch or I'm obnoxious, 'cos I am.**❞** **COURTNEY, 1992**

❝I usually just take the J Mascis (Dinosaur Jr.) Fifth Amendment and say nothing. I personally don't care what my favourite band's music is about or what their personal interests are. It usually just affects me musically. I mean, they could be speaking in tongues and it wouldn't matter to me as long as it sounds good.❞

KURT ON INTERVIEWS, 1992

"The biggest 'Fuck you' of my life goes out to the self-inflated, indefensible, florid and pompous lies set down by Lynn Hirschberg and any lemming that followed her, knowing how evil and how full of shit her story was. I think it's very sad that we can't move onward in the history/demise of rock music instead of assigning me/us/my wife these ridiculous, archetypal, retro rock roles to live out. We are decent, ethical people – we take no delight in being involved in blatant sexism, treachery, or scandals made up off the top of someone's head. And now, as a result of Ms Hirschberg's personal and unhealthy obsession with me/us/my wife, we are having to deal with the betrayal and harassment that stems from the 'inside sources' and aspiring groupie 'writers' who surround us now like celebrity worshipping jackals moving in for the kill.

I have learned one thing from this and not much else – the life of a failed groupie (i.e. someone with no self-respect but a hugely sociopathic need to be near to and be accepted by successful people, whether the objects of their obsessions like them or not) is a very sad and dangerous thing. I'd really like to thank those of you in the media who saw this for what it was and did not sell us down the river for the sake of a 'story', who didn't dirty our music with things that have nothing to do with music or, for that matter, reality.

Let's see what else I can complain about... oh yeah – I don't feel the least bit guilty for commercially exploiting a completely exhausted rock youth culture because, at this point in rock history, punk rock (while still sacred to some) is, to me, dead gone. We just wanted to pay tribute to something that helped us to feel as though we had crawled out of the

MEDIA, PRIVACY & GOOD BEHAVIOUR "

dung heap of conformity. To pay tribute like an Elvis or Jimi Hendrix impersonator in the tradition of a bar band. I'll be the first to admit that we're the Nineties version of Cheap Trick or The Knack, but the last to admit that it hasn't been rewarding.

At this point. I have a request for our fans. If any of you in any way hate homosexuals, people of different colour, or women, please do this one favour for us – leave us the fuck alone! Don't come to our shows, and don't buy our records. **"**

SCATHING ATTACK BY KURT ON LYNN (*VANITY FAIR*) HIRSCHBERG THAT WAS TO BE INCLUDED IN THE ORIGINAL SLEEVE NOTES TO *INCESTICIDE* BUT THEN CUT AT THE LAST MINUTE.

"There were like 60 sarcastic things I told *Vanity Fair*, that they quoted straight because they're so stupid. Their whole attitude was like, 'Let's go and be condescending to these wacky punk rock kids and make allusions to how, in their world, success is bad. Aren't they cute?'" COURTNEY, 1993

"I think Courtney and I have said too many things at times, or said some unnecessary things. We're just learning like everyone else. But I think it's unhealthy to read all this negative stuff and I do try to ignore it as much as I can.

There are a lot of times when Courtney'll say, 'OK, here's another one', and start reading it and I'll just walk out of the room. It affects me only because it affects her more. She's not made of stone, she's not what's been written about her, she has emotions and feelings like everyone else and it really upsets her. And she's constantly combating this stuff, trying to clear it up. **"**

KURT, 1993

" Really, after all the shit I've had to read about me and especially my wife – in the last year and a half, I should've put out a really hateful record. I should've used every chance I had to attack people I wanted to, I feel that strongly about it, but there's just no point. I'm already known as a cry-baby whiner. **"** KURT, 1993

" She (Courtney) has a pretty good idea how the media works and stuff. I've never really paid attention to it. No, I'd never think of boring my friends complaining about shit like that. **"** **KURT, 1993**

" I've suffered on a large scale but most of the attacks haven't been on me, they've been on someone I'm totally in love with, my best fucking friend is being completely fucking crucified every two months, if not more. I read a negative article about her every two months. A lot of the time I can't escape it because Courtney gets faxes of articles from the publicist all the time. But also it's a form of protection. It enables you to remember who has fucked you and to make sure you never deal with those people again. And another reason we like to read it is that we can learn from the criticism, too. If I never read any of the interviews I did, I'd never be able to say, 'Jeez, that was a really stupid thing to say. I'd better try to clear that up'. **"** KURT, 1993

MEDIA, PRIVACY & **GOOD BEHAVIOUR**

"I think the only reason we've ever had a reputation for being a negative band was because of the articles written about us, addressing the drug use and stuff. Like, we've been accused of inciting people to drop out of society. But if we do that it's not in a lazy way. I mean, I've always thought of us attacking that slacker stuff. But we *have* pointed out things about society that's not good and I know some people don't like that, they think it's dangerous. And I think that's why they fuck with us.**"** KURT, 1993

"Remember, if you write anything nasty about me, I'll come round and blow up your toilet." COURTNEY, 1994

"I still see stuff, descriptions of rock-stars in some magazine – 'Sting, the environmental mental guy', and 'Kurt Cobain, the whiny, complaining, neurotic, bitchy guy who hates everything, hates rock-stardom, hates his life'. And I've never been happier in my life. I'm a much happier guy than a lot of people think.**"** KURT, 1994

"It's the lying I can't stand. It's the lying that gets me down. One thing this last terrible year has proved: if you lie about us, I will hit you. Kurt will shoot you and we will sue." COURTNEY, 1994

"I had this theory that the persona people project onstage is the exact opposite of who they are. In Kurt's case, it was 'Fuck you!' And ultimately his largest problem in life was not being able to say, 'Fuck you'. In real life, real real life, I'm supersensitive. But people tend to think I'm not vulnerable because I don't act vulnerable.**"**
COURTNEY, 1994

"All I have to do is lick my finger, stick it up in the air, and shit sticks to it." COURTNEY, 1995

"I go to a bar and I leave, and I know that no matter how quiet I've been or what I haven't done, for the next week it'll be spoken of that I came in and yelled and fucked whoever on the floor.**"**
COURTNEY, 1995

"The frenetic outside world was the enemy, horrifying. I'd try and get Kurt to stop reading things about himself; I wouldn't buy him magazines any more. But he'd sneak off and buy them. He got addicted. Every jibe, every caricature, every reference. This was someone who couldn't deal with being paraphrased wrongly. So be it the cultural reference for every fucking thing there was... and this was someone who had been pretty much unnoticed most of his life. He wanted to be popular, very much a people pleaser. He found a hidden stash of magazines that I put away, about three months' worth. And we got into a physical fight. I was trying to tear them away. He was ripping pages out on the floor. He was like a cornered animal. He hit out a me – 'Get away, get away'. I couldn't stop him. I tried to say to him: 'It's a cloud, it'll pass'. 'Damn right, it'll pass. I'm not gonna make any fucking music every again. I'm not gonna fucking be here to see it pass'. The usual stuff he would say." COURTNEY ON KURT AND THE MEDIA, 1994

Air Rage

"I cussed at a lady – my daughter always said I had a potty mouth. I cussed at a lady named Mary, she wasn't letting my friend into first class, and I said 'Why are you being such a bitch about it?'" **COURTNEY, BEING RELEASED FROM HEATHROW POLICE STATION WITH A CAUTION, 2003**

"I've no regrets about what happened. The stewardess was a bitch. It seems it is a crime in this country to cuss." COURTNEY, 2003

"I wasn't drunk. I wasn't close to being inebriated. Nothing. I had half a glass of champagne on take-off. It was absolutely over nothing. This happened to me once in Australia. I'm literally blameless. It was a real exhausting waste of time and I really wanted to come over here and be a pro, no shenanigans."

COURTNEY, 2003

RICHARD BRANSON

"If (Richard) Branson's here he's going to get a smack in the mouth." COURTNEY AT AN EAST LONDON PARTY, 2003

"Everything with Richard (Branson) and I is great, we're getting on fine. He's a really nice guy and quite cute, I've taken to him. He's even given me four free VIP flights on his plane. It's great.**"**

COURTNEY, 2003

"Courtney came through and sat on my friend's lap and started talking about how she wanted to buy a house in London. She was pretty off it, but not particularly rude. The staff seemed a bit stuck up, and took it all a bit too seriously."

FELLOW PASSENGER ON THE VIRGIN ATLANTIC AIRLINER, 2003

"We will not tolerate improper behaviour by passengers on board any of our aircraft and always press for prosecution of passenger charged with unruly behaviour. The safety of all our passengers and crew is of paramount importance.**"**

VIRGIN ATLANTIC AIRLINES SPOKESPERSON, 2003

"She is the epitome of rock and roll, like a female version of a young Johnny Rotten – we're a rock and roll airline. She has accepted she acted a little badly and is welcome on our planes any time – in fact she's flying back to LA first class next week."

RICHARD BRANSON, 2003

"I was going to give her a little slap on the bottom for being a bad girl but I started chatting to her and we really hit it off.**"**

RICHARD BRANSON, 2003

MEDIA, PRIVACY & GOOD BEHAVIOUR ,,

Kurt's Death

Guns

"We were jamming in the garage, Kurt was on drums, and a neighbour called the cops. Six cops arrived and we started arguing when they asked us if we had any guns in the house. Kurt said no and I said yes, and we began to fight, so the cops arrested Kurt. I don't want guns in the house, maybe one but not three. We hardly ever fight... no-one could ask for a better husband. He went on the cover of *The Advocate* (a national US gay and lesbian mag). He's a feminist." **COURTNEY**

"I like guns. I just enjoy shooting them." KURT, 1994

"It's protection. I don't have bodyguards. There are people way less famous than I am or Courtney who have been stalked and murdered. It could be someone by chance looking for a house to break into. We have a security system. I actually have one gun that is loaded but I keep it safe, in a cabinet high up on a shelf where Frances can never get to it. And I have an M16, which is fun to shoot. It's the only sport I have every liked. It's not something I'm obsessed with or even condone. I don't really think much of it. Look, I'm not a very physical person. I wouldn't be able to stop an intruder who had a gun or a knife. But I'm not going to stand by and watch my family stabbed to death or raped in front of me. I wouldn't think twice of blowing someone's head off if they did that. It's for protection reasons. And sometimes it's fun to go out and shoot. At targets. I want to make that clear." **KURT, 1994**

"His whole thing was, 'I'm only alive because of Frances and you'. Look at his interviews. In each and every one he mentions blowing his head off. He brought a gun to the hospital the day after our daughter was born. He was going to Reading the next morning. I was like, 'I'll go first'. I held this thing in my hand... And what about Frances? Sort of rude. 'Oh, your parents died the day after you were born'. And I just started talking him out of it. And he said, 'Fuck you, you can't chicken out. I'm gonna do it'. But I made him give me the gun." COURTNEY, 1994

"He totally fucking lied to you. He never went shooting in his life. One time he said, 'I'm going shooting'. Yeah. Shooting what? He never even made it to the range. Yeah, it was an issue in the house. I like having a revolver for protection. But when he bought the Uzi thing... 'Hey, is that a toy, Kurt?' Yeah, it's dangerous when you're dealing with two volatile people – one is clinically depressed and the other one is suicidal at moments and definitely co-dependent." **COURTNEY, 1994**

"The reason I flipped out on March 18 was because it had been six days since we came back from Rome, and I couldn't take it any more. When he came back from Rome high, I flipped out. If there's one thing in my whole life I could take back, it would be that. Getting mad at him for coming home high. I wish to God I hadn't. I wish I'd just been the way I always was, just tolerant of it. It made him feel so worthless when I got mad at him."

COURTNEY, 1994

KURT'S DEATH

❝He said, 'No matter what happens, I want you to know that you made a really good record (*Live Though This* was due to be released 11 days later). 'I said, 'Well what do you mean?' And he said, 'Just remember, no matter what, I love you'.❞

COURTNEY RECALLING THE LAST TIME SHE SPOKE TO KURT BEFORE HE TOOK HIS LIFE WITH A SHOTGUN

❝**He's probably going to turn up dead and join that stupid club.**❞

WENDY O'CONNOR, KURT'S MOTHER, REFERRING TO ROCK STARS WHO HAD KILLED THEMSELVES. HOURS LATER KURT'S BODY WAS FOUND

❝I haven't felt excitement in listening to as well as creating for too many years now. I feel guilty beyond words about these things. For example, when we're backstage and the lights go out, and the manic roar of the crowd begins, it doesn't affect me the way it did for, say Freddie Mercury, who seemed to have loved and relished the adoration of the crowd. This is something I totally admire and envy. The fact is, I can't fool you, any of you. It simply isn't fair to you or me. The worst crime I can think of would be to put people off by faking it and pretending as if I was having 100% fun. Sometimes I feel as if I should have a punch- in time clock before I walk out on stage. I've tried everything within my power to appreciate the fact that I/we have affected and entertained a lot of people.

I must be one of those narcissists who only enjoy things when they're alone. I'm too sensitive. Oh, I need to be slightly numb in order to regain the enthusiasm I once had as a child.
On our last three tours, I had a much better appreciation of all the people I've known personally and fans of our music. But I still can't get out the frustration, the guilt and the empathy I have for everybody.

There is good in all of us, and I simply love people too much. So much that it makes me feel too... sad – sad, little, sensitive, unappreciated, Pisces Jesus Man. And I had it good, very good. I'm grateful. But since the age of seven, I've become hateful towards all humans in general... only because I love and feel for people too much, I guess. I thank you all from the pit of my burning nauseous stomach for your letters and concern over the last years. I'm too much of an erratic, moody person that I don't have the passion any more. So remember, it's better to burn out than fade away.
Peace. Love. Empathy. Kurt Cobain**" KURT'S SUICIDE NOTE, APRIL 1994**

"It was the sweetest note." COURTNEY, APRIL 1994

"He wrote me a letter other than his suicide note. It's kind of long. I put it in a safe-deposit box. I might show it to Frances... maybe. It's very fucked up writing. 'You know I love you, I love Frances, I'm so sorry. Please don't follow me'. It's long because he repeats himself. 'I'm sorry, I'm sorry, I'm sorry. I'll be there, I'll protect you. I don't know where I'm going. I just can't be here anymore'.

There's definitely a narcissism in what he did, too. It was very snotty of him. When we decided we were in love at the Beverley Garland Hotel, we found this dead bird. Took out three feathers. And he said, 'This is for you, this is for me, and this is for our baby we're gonna have'. And he took one of the feathers away."

COURTNEY, 1994

KURT'S DEATH

"I lived with someone who every day said they were going to kill himself, and it wasn't like I was bored with it by any means. I did what I could to make sure that didn't happen. And that resulted in a lot of hysteria on my part. There was a lot of screaming, a lot of yelling. A lot of kicking the walls, a lot of broken fax machines and telephones. I started to feel like my purpose in life was noble – to take care of these two human beings, my husband and child, and make sure that they lived. And it was a fine purpose. I didn't have a problem with that." COURTNEY, 1994

"At first I thought it was a mannequin and then I noticed it had blood in the right ear. Then I saw a shotgun lying across his chest, pointed up at his chest.**"**

GARY SMITH, ELECTRICIAN WHO FOUND KURT'S BODY, APRIL 1994

"I walked around to the door on the back side of the garage. I looked to see if I had a way to route the wire, and saw the body through a glass opening in a door. At night, I'll be lying there and the scene keeps flashing over and over again. I have a four year old son, so it makes me think of the little girl he left behind."

GARY SMITH

"I didn't know where he was. He never, ever disappeared like that. He always called me.**" COURTNEY, APRIL 1994**

"Just blaming it (Kurt's suicide) on smack is stupid. People have been taking smack for a hundred years. You can get smack in any town. This is just a Tonya Harding thing... all this talk about Seattle and smack. Smack was just a small part of his life."

KRIST NOVOSELIC, APRIL 1994

"I listened to too many people (telling her different ways to prevent Kurt from taking his own life). I'm only going to listen to my gut for the rest of my life. It's all my fault. I'm tough and I can take anything. But I can't take this.**" COURTNEY, APRIL 1994**

"The only thing I can call it was a downward spiral from there. I got angry, and it was for the first time I ever had. And I'm sorry – wherever the hell he is. And when people say, 'Where was she, where was she?' I was in LA because the interventionist said I had to leave. Interventionist walks in to the house; 'Dominant female, get rid of her'. I did not even kiss or get to say goodbye to my husband. I wish to God... Kurt thought I was on their side because I had gone along with them. I wasn't. I was afraid."

COURTNEY, REFLECTING ON THE SUBJECT OF INTERVENTION ON KURT'S DEATH

"Everyone who feels guilty, raise your hand."

COURTNEY ON MTV, APRIL 1994

"How could I not (think one day he was going to kill himself) when he talked about it every single day? If there were 99 dots on the wall, he was going to kill himself. If such and such happened that day he was going to kill himself." COURTNEY, 1995

"I flipped out because he was absolutely crazy. Out of his tree. I was desperate. So I called an intervention. And they wouldn't even let me stick around. They had a Lear jet waiting for me." **COURTNEY, 1995**

"It was on April 2. There was a block on the phone for everybody but him. I did not sleep. I called the operator every couple of hours to make sure, in case they changed shifts. They all knew that if Mr. Cobain called, put that fucking call through to me. 8:54 A.M. I was not asleep. He called and for six minutes he tried to get through, and could not. For him to argue for six minutes on the phone is crazed. I cannot imagine him arguing for six minutes. He did though. And what that told him is that I was on their side. That I had a block on the phone for him. And I did not. Kurt's whole plan was to wear everybody down, but he could never wear me down. I think, though, at that very moment he thought I had given up on him." COURTNEY, 1995

"He's gone. There's no ghost in here. The only thing that would make him hang around is guilt, and I don't want him to feel that."
COURTNEY'S WORDS AS SHE SHOWS AN INSIDER INTO THE SMALL ROOM
WHERE KURT SHOT HIMSELF, 1995

"I said if he ever lived to be 30, I'd be surprised."
WENDY O'CONNOR, KURT'S MOTHER

"Some of Kurt's ashes will be buried in a public cemetery, some are underneath the Budda in my bedroom, some are in the alter in the living room, and some more of Kurt – not a great amount – is in India, being made into a stupa (a shrine blessed by His Holiness the Dalai Lama). For the stupa you get to pick a place and a deity. The place I picked is Nirvana, and the deity is a minor god. He's a small man, and he has this really large diamond that he is holding, and the diamond is so big that it keeps knocking him over. The diamond is far too heavy a burden for him." COURTNEY, 1995

"Calls have almost doubled. Most people say they know how Kurt felt. We fear some fans may think it's cool to follow him to an early grave." NEW YORK SAMARITANS, APRIL 1994

KURT'S DEATH

Kurt's
Legacy

"I'm a spokesman for myself. It just so happens that there's a bunch of people that are concerned with what I have to say. I find that frightening at times because I'm just as confused as most people. I don't have answers for anything, I don't want to be a fucking spokesperson." **KURT, 1992**

"I'm not going to play the Yoko thing. I'm not going to be the keeper of the flame." COURTNEY, 1994

"I'm not leaving this house (the family house in which Kurt died). This is the house that Kurt wanted us to have." **COURTNEY, 1994**

"Imagine this: You're peaking. You're in your youth. At the prime of your life. The last thing you want to be is a symbol of heroin use. You've finally met up with somebody of the opposite gender who you can write with. That's never happened before in your life. The only other person you could ever write with wasn't as good a writer as you, and this person's a better writer than you. And you're in love, you have a best friend, you have a soul-fucking mate, and you can't believe it's happening in your lifetime. And as a bonus he's beautiful. *And* he's rich. And as a bonus he's a hot rock star to boot. *And* he's the best fuck that ever walked. And he wants to have babies, and what you want is babies. You've wanted to have babies forever. *And* he understands everything you say. And he completes your sentences. And he's lazy but he's spiritual, and he's not embarrassed about praying, he's not embarrassed about chanting, he's not embarrassed about God, Jesus none of it. He fucking thinks it's all really cool. He wants to

KURT & **COURTNEY** *Talking*

66 fucking learn the path. He wants to be enlightened. Everything. And there's even room for you to fix him, which you like, 'cause your a fixer-upper. He's perfect in almost every way. The only fucking happiness that I ever had. And then it all gets taken away... 99 COURTNEY, ON HER LIFE WITH KURT

66 There are issues between me, Krist and Dave that need to be resolved. But I want the lines of communication to be open. For Frances sake as much as mine. 99 **COURTNEY, 1994**

66 I'd describe them as slightly tense, but good. Our intentions toward each other are really positive. There's not some horrible Yoko nightmare going on, and hopefully there never will be. I totally respect Krist's feelings for Kurt and the way he's handled himself since Kurt's death. One thing Kurt told me a long time ago, and he made very clear, was that no matter what mood he was in with Krist, he and Krist had the exact same taste in music. 99 COURTNEY ON RELATIONS BETWEEN HER AND THE REMAINING
MEMBERS OF NIRVANA, 1995

66 Sogyal Rinpoche's *The Tibetan Book of Living and Dying* has a detailed description of what happens when you die, and how you can help a dead person. That's really important to me: having control over the destiny of Kurt in terms of his spirit, where he was, and where he's destined to be. I just thought I had everything that I wanted, and I didn't need to chant any more. I'll tell you this right now... period, guaranteed, end of story... if I had not stopped chanting Kurt would still be here. 99
COURTNEY AND HER FAITH IN BUDDHISM

66 I have disappointing news. I have no intention of dying young and being some stinking rock n' roll person. In years to come I'm gonna be a matriarch with a big brood. I'd like to have an incredibly big garden and a potty old husband who sits and paints. I'd like to just sit and watch the sun, and when I'm on my death bed, I'll be thinking about my husband and my baby, nothing else. 99 COURTNEY, 1995

The Future They Once Had

❝ But I'd also like to have a side project. When you've been working with the same people for a while there's not much not more you can do, even though I feel we've succeeded in coming up with some new styles. It'd be fun to play with someone else. But every time I do that, I end up regretting it. Because, if it sounds good, I wish that Nirvana had done it. **❞** KURT, 1992

❝ It's impossible for me to look into the future and say I'm going to be able to play Nirvana songs in 10 years. There's no way. I don't want to resort to doing the Eric Clapton thing. Not to put him down whatsoever; I have immense respect for him. But I don't want to have to change the songs to fit my age. ❞ KURT, 1994

❝ I can't say that I've heard a band who sounds like they ripped us off. I hope they have just been influenced by the sincerity that we try to pull off. **❞** KURT

KURT & **COURTNEY** *Talking* **❞❞**

❝I hate to even say it, but I can't see this band lasting more than a couple of albums, unless we work really hard on experimenting. I mean let's face it. When the same people are together doing the same job, they're limited. I'm really interested in studying different things, and I know Krist and Dave are as well. But I don't know if we are capable of doing it together. I don't want to put out another record that sounds like the last three records.**❞**

KURT, 1994

❝My goal keeps me alive. And no personal issue is going to interfere with that. If people try to put me in the crazy box – 'crazy fucking Courtney' – go ahead. But if you think you're going to stop me from where I'm going, you're not going to do it. I work my ass off. I delivery the goddamn goods. And I will delivery them again.**❞**

COURTNEY, 1994

❝I used to be able to talk to Kurt more, wherever he is. But now he's really gone. I used to feel like mourning him was really selfish because it would make him feel guilty. And the best thing to do was to pray for him and show him joy, so he could feel the vibration of the joy. But now I know he's dissipated, and he's gone. There's not anything left. Not even to talk to.**❞**

COURTNEY, 1994

Legal Matters

"Nirvana could never be a partnership because it was the living manifestation of the creative vision, personal will, and life force of a single unique individual."

COURTNEY, IN A COURT DEPOSITION ON THE '97 PARTNERSHIP AGREEMENT BETWEEN THE COBAIN ESTATE AND KRIST NOVOSELIC AND DAVE GROHL, 2000

"I'm an artist and a good artist I think, but I'm not an artist that has to play all the time and thus has to get fucked. Maybe my laziness and self-destructive streak will finally pay off and serve a community desperately in need of it. They can't torture me like they could Lucinda Williams."

COURTNEY OUTLINING HER ARGUMENT WITH UNIVERSAL MUSIC, 2000

"I've spent a long and hard two years fighting this lawsuit, a vast amount of money, and I am about to be responsible for turning around a labour law that will affect all artists in America and hopefully become standard in the UK as well. Not to mention that I've put enormous money and effort into starting a union which, like the ones for actors and athletes, would provide retirement, childcare, healthcare, alcohol and drug rehabilitation, and everything else that even a make-up artist gets in the film business. And I've also managed to write some great songs along the way." COURTNEY, 2001

"This is not a renegotiation. The contract itself needs to change; it's impossible to mend. If I have to stand alone, I'll stand alone. I love fighting. I wake up every day rich. I wake up every day with a movie career. I've got three movies lined up. I'm this weird ex-stripper-junkie, and I don't give a shit. If I don't do this, who can?" COURTNEY, 2001

KURT & **COURTNEY** *Talking*

"I feel a spiritual commitment, due to the fact that I inherited a lot of Kurt's money. My daughter has most of it, but I have some. There's some sort of deliverance in doing this. It would honour him. I own the Nirvana catalogue, and I'm doing what I think is right by my husband. Part of it is closure on that, too."

COURTNEY, 2001

"I could end up being the music industry's worst nightmare, a smart gal with a fat bank account who it unafraid to go down in flames fighting for a principle." COURTNEY, 2001

"I never picked on harmless people. I've always picked on people I felt were corrupt or more corrupt than me." **COURTNEY, 2001**

"It's incredibly easy not to be a musician. It's always a struggle and a dangerous career choice. We are motivated by passion and money. That's not a dirty little secret. It's a fact. Take away the incentive for major or minor financial reward and you dilute the pool of musicians." COURTNEY, 2000

"I'm gonna win that case in about four hours."

COURTNEY ON HER LEGAL BATTLE, 2002

"You'll get the new Nirvana record at Christmas... we love each other now. We're getting along fine." COURTNEY, 2002

"We hope that this (greatest-hits) release will enable long-time Nirvana fans to hear some of their favourite songs in a new context. At the same time, the upcoming CD will allow a whole new audience to appreciate Nirvana's music and Kurt Cobain's great talent." JOINT STATEMENT FROM COURTNEY, GROHL AND NOVOSELIC, 2002

Acting Up

"I guess it's really a desperate need for attention or something, when I was younger, when I was a kid, I did a lot of acting and then there was this really pathetic phase in the early Eighties; my actress phase, but I don't want to talk about it. It was a year and then I went back to start another band. But I've always looked at scripts and wanted to be in them." COURTNEY, 1997

"**It's much better than music. You don't have to go play a traditional role. In film it's a little more constrained; you're not supposed to say 'feminist' out loud I guess.**" COURTNEY, 1997

"I always thought it was kind of lame to do both (music and acting), but it's me so... I've done things that people said couldn't be done, so I'm not really that concerned with whether something can be done or not because you just kind of do it, don't you? And if you're good at it, then good for you." COURTNEY, 1997

"**You have to have an inner integrity meter. The humanity around actors in the film community, because of Darwinism, because of commerce, is so much more than in rock. I mean, you need your actors to be good-looking, spiritually grounded, healthy. They need to have outside pursuits, they need to be healthy human beings so when they go do drugs, everyone just ignores it. But in this business, y'know, you want your rock stars to have problems. You need them to have bad skin.**"

COURTNEY, 1998

COURTNEY WITH DREW BARRYMORE

KURT & **COURTNEY** *Talking*

❝With film you can change things, you can alter the skyline so much. You can change the culture...❞ **COURTNEY, 1999**

❝I know how to embrace the mainstream for a movie. I did that once and I was totally OK with it. There's rules and regulations. You're just selling the movie. it's basic. But in music, it's so much more complex and so much about what I have to say. I'm the director. It's my thing with my band. So I feel a little more me and I get mad at them and I don't wanna get mad at them. I wanna embrace them and I wanna feel happy about achieving something that I really want. And I wanna be used for the purpose that I'm here for.❞ COURTNEY, 1999

❝This year, myself and a partner are going to start a production company as well, not so much for projects for me to act in, but more based on the model of what he's doing, what Drew Barrymore's doing, what Danny DeVito's doing. I mean, I wanna see coming-of-age films which are great. I wanna use my taste, which I've honed and honed, to affect that medium. I mean, these are shadows and light on a screen and yet in some ways they can be more effective and more refined than a great pop song.❞
COURTNEY, 1999

❝I'm a solid part of the (Hollywood) community. I don't always get the jobs I want, but I'm getting them more and more lately. It doesn't hurt that I was Milos Forman's 'discovery' and that my grandmother Paula Fox just published her memoirs and revealed that my great-uncle was Douglas Fairbanks. I got more calls on that than you could imagine. 'I always knew you had royal blood,' etc etc. It was like, OK, so what if my name had been Courtney Fairbanks my whole life... Look what male identification does to you. If I had gotten the name, I would probably have been stuck on some magazine cover at 18 and never even gotten to play rock.❞ COURTNEY, 2001

The People Vs
Larry Flynt (1996)

"He (Flynt) has become my friend. I don't like his job, but my roadies read his magazines." **COURTNEY, 1997**

"I had to lose weight for this film, and ate no carbohydrates for three weeks. Terrible for the body, but I lost 30lb." COURTNEY, 1997

"I read a lot of *Hustlers* and they are pretty gross. But it is a folk art, and the way Flynt makes money." **COURTNEY, 1997**

"Because of my drugs past the film studio had refused to insure me. The director, Milos Forman, supported me, and I ended up paying a huge amount of money – well over $1 million – to an insurance company in case I messed up. I got the money back only after I completed the film." COURTNEY, 1997

WITH WOODY HARRELSON IN *THE PEOPLE VS. LARRY FLINT*

ACTING UP

"I got mad at that (having to take a weekly urine test)... but it was to make sure I was really off drugs.**"** COURTNEY, 1997

"I have had a lot of support from my daughter, Frances. She is only four, but she's like angel cake on earth. She inspires me more than anyone."
COURTNEY, 1997

"I don't think women get aroused by the sight of naked flesh in the same way as men. It is more subtle. I like sexual tension, without the obvious; I need thoughts, not pictures.**"** COURTNEY, 1997

"I refused to be totally naked, apart from the death scene... I am being hypocritical here, because it is a movie about a porn publisher. But my scenes were not really sexual or erotic. And, as the daughter of hippie parents, I know there are worse things than being seen naked in a movie." COURTNEY, 1997

"I like Larry (Flynt). He's done some good things for me and he's a nice guy. He's got a code of honour when it comes to people that are close to him.**"** COURTNEY, 1997

"The character was somebody that I could probably get, that I could bring something to. But it was mostly Milos Forman. I think he's one of the greatest living film-makers and primarily because, even in the films that a lot of us haven't seen like *The Fireman's Ball*, he has a great love for humanity. Very irreverent, not very

furious, not very angry, but he can portray things very wickedly and I loved that. And I love that he can bring something to this issue of censorship." COURTNEY, 1997

"Well, (the porn industry) is billions and billions of dollars a year that men make by basically turning women into currency, and although we vilify women who do it, I wish it was the women who were getting the money. Not that I would agree with a women who was doing it... I like more sort of high-end porn ladies, like *The English Patient* or something. I think it should be a different kind of industry because it's not going to go away." **COURTNEY, 1997**

"I don't care, it wasn't my turn yet. I'm from the rock world – we don't get recognised the first time out."

COURTNEY ON HER OMISSION FROM OSCAR NOMINATIONS, 1997

200 Cigarettes (1999)

"In acting you take your chances a little more. I mean, I did an ensemble piece called *200 Cigarettes* that I have no idea if it's good or not. I hear mixed things about it. I have quality control over the music thing and, as a producer, I will have quality control over films but , as an actress, I'm not in charge of my craft."

COURTNEY, 1999

Man On The Moon (2000)

"What's so weird is that 'Man On The Moon' was Kurt's absolute favourite song of R.E.M.'s and I was more old-school R.E.M., which I thought was interesting. I'm comfortable bringing it up, it doesn't bother me. I like that aspect of it, I like the cycle of karma of it. I like that it was Milos and it was random and it was pretty much my two favourite men..." **COURTNEY, 1999**

ACTING UP

Courtney's Solo Music

America's Sweetheart

"There's a new song, 'Life Despite God', which literally described planes hitting buildings and apocalyptic dreamscape city – weeks before September 11, as morbid as that is. I know I'm in the flow when my lyrics start getting psychic and dream-connected again.**"**

COURTNEY, 2001

"This song is a great way to start a show."

COURTNEY ON 'ALL THE DRUGS IN THE WORLD', 2003

"(The new album's) deeply, deeply spiritual, it's much less polished than anything on *Celebrity Skin* but catchy nonetheless.**"**

COURTNEY, 2003

"You'd better get a lyric you can live with forever. There's a lyric in there which is 'I am the centre of the universe,' and I get to say that every fucking night. When I say it I have no problems, because I get to sing, 'I am the centre of the FUCKING universe.'**"** COURTNEY, 2003

"I have a cassette of me and Liam (Gallagher) and he did the 'Songbird' song. And I was whistling. If he's not going to do it, I'm fucking doing it. Mine has him whistling, it's awesome. Somebody should bootleg that!" COURTNEY, 2003

"I'm gonna have a top five record over there (in Britain) within two months. I'll put those little Strokes in their place." COURTNEY, 2002

"I want to pass that two million mark. I want enough material that I can kick anyone's ass." COURTNEY, 2003

"Women Required for International Rock Revolution! Join Courtney Love's Touring Band and get famous, see the world! Must play BASS or GUITAR (Really Play) and look like a Goddess. We like Emily the Strange, Lolita Goth, Patty Schemel's drumming, *Nuggets* and *Performance* the Movie. We love Flea but don't want you to play like him. We start NOW. NO BOYS."

ADVERT IN US MAGAZINE *VILLAGE VOICE*, 2003

COURTNEY'S SOLO MUSIC

After Kurt

❝There's gonna be a marble gravestone with an angel on top and a line from 'Dump'. That's why it's taken a year to get the gravestone just right.❞ **COURTNEY, 1995**

❝**They (Mudhoney) never sent flowers. They never came to the funeral, even though they were playing 40 miles away.**❞

COURTNEY, 1995

❝One of the misconceptions about my husband was that he was so fucked up – that he was passive. He wore the pants in a big way.❞

COURTNEY, 1995

❝**I don't know, this whole subject of sleeping with people and going out with somebody – it's been a weird year. A few months ago I really began to 'see the world', so to speak.**❞ COURTNEY, 1995

❝I let men be men, I should let people know this so I won't have all these wimpy little boys chasing after me any more. They keep thinking I'm going to beat the shit out of them.❞ **COURTNEY, 1995**

❝**I've always love frail men. I've never liked macho guys. I've only ever gone out with frail men.**❞ COURTNEY, 1996

❝I was incredibly suicidal for the first few months after Kurt's death, but in the middle of it all, I remembered that I had a daughter. I'm much calmer now.❞ **COURTNEY, 1999**

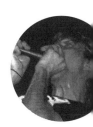

Mellowing Out?

"When I talk about making up, I don't mean with people like Lynn Hirschberg, who I'll never forgive for writing that *Vanity Fair* piece (claiming Courtney was using heroin whilst pregnant). I went to the Oscars with Amanda De Cadenet – and I don't give a shit what anyone says about her, she's really cool – and Tarantino was sitting between me and Lynn. Not killing her was a milestone for me. I could have hit her with Tarantino's Oscar..." **COURTNEY, 1995**

"**I'm a Buddhist, so I always look for somewhere spiritual which clears my head.**" COURTNEY, 1997

"I need reassurance just like everyone else." **COURTNEY, 1997**

"**So soothing. It's better than drugs. I've watched every single episode except the first season, which was in black and white. It's soothing and wonderful and great. And the English class system from 1912 to 1924... so fascinating.**"
COURTNEY ON WATCHING ENGLISH TV'S *UPSTAIRS DOWNSTAIRS*, 1999

"I want to move into Jagger's old place on Cheyne Walk, that's top of my list. It's a really cool house." **COURTNEY ON UK HOUSE-HUNTING, 2003**

"**My notorious reputation is a bit of a fantasy. Anyone who works with me will attest that I'm very professional.**" COURTNEY, 1999

"Have I gone LA? Dude! Scientology acupuncture raw foods apple fasts Pilates coffee colonics essential cocaine oil deep tissue massage escort service porno goddess punk singer Pakistani poppy tea... Yeah, bring it on! I *am* LA!" **COURTNEY, 2001**

KURT & **COURTNEY** *Talking*

What They Said About Kurt & Courtney

66 It was in 1987, at his apartment, which was loaded up with a lot of thrift-store knick-knacks, huge posters of Queen and The Rolling Stones, and little cages with pets everywhere. And I remember distinctly his pet rat bit me and I screamed quite loudly. I remember thinking he seemed kind of like an Eighties idea of a beatnik. The guy was obviously not spending a lot of time at work, and was just kind of living on a thrift-store aesthetic. 99

BRUCE PAVITT, CO-OWNER AND FOUNDER OF SUB-POP RECORDS, RECALLING THE FIRST TIME HE MET KURT

66 **Kurt was terrified of jocks and moron dudes.** 99

MATT LUKIN FROM MUDHONEY

66 In the spring of '89, Nirvana played a show at the community centre in my hometown of Ellensburg, Washington. They completely blew me away; it was like seeing The Who in their prime. After two songs some jerk who worked there stopped the show... they'd gone over their time limit because the ten local bands who had opened had gone over time. So they just stood there for a second and then Krist started throwing his bass in the air, up to the top of this 20 foot ceiling, and catching it with one hand. Meanwhile Kurt was letting his amp go loud as hell, and

their road manager got in a fist fight with the jerk guy. The whole thing was crazed, And this was in Ellensburg, of all places. I still believe to this day that it's the best fucking band I have ever seen. And I miss the guy (Kurt) more than I could ever express. **"** **MARK LANEGAN, SCREAMING TREES**

"Hypnotic and righteous heaviness from these Olympia pop stars. They're young, they own their own van, and they're going to make us rich!" SUB-POP PRESS RELEASE FOR 'IN BLOOM'.

" May or June 1991, Jabberjaw, Los Angeles. A spur-of-the moment show during the making of *Nevermind*. About 400 lucky souls crammed into this dingy, dinky art space to sweat and stink as one. Every rock voyeur and band geek in town was there to hear, for the first time, the songs that would be *Nevermind*. The show was a mess, but, as always, Nirvana's wild yet child-sweet spirit filled the room. I remember somehow deciphering parts of 'Smells Like Teen Spirit' and 'Lithium' out of the noise and confusion and feeling overwhelmed. Nirvana were beautiful like no other. **"**

HOLE'S ERIC ERLANDSON ON HIS FONDEST MEMORY OF KURT AND NIRVANA

"He was unhappy before he was famous, and he was unhappy after he was famous. He was just unhappy."

NIRVANA MANAGER DANNY GOLDBERG ON KURT

" The most anti-authority guy I know is Kurt. He'll be the one to walk up to people and scream, 'Why? Why? Why?' A lot of times I'll understand the reason behind things, even if I don't agree with it. Kurt's the guy out there yelling at the top of his lungs. **"**

KRIST NOVOSELIC, 1992

"I think underground music should stay underground. Like, Nirvana were one of my favourite bands. But now the whole thing's kind of a drag. I don't even want to put on a Nirvana record any more. 'Teen Spirit' is a great song. But when I hear jerks, like jock bozos or something, talking about it, I get real sad. I guess I don't like it that they've got that kind of audience. It's really irritating that somehow all these dumb jocks are getting into it. In a sense Nirvana are a new kind of icon." KIM GORDON, SONIC YOUTH, 1992

KIM GORDON

"That ambiguity, that the whole thing. What the kids are attracted to in the music is that he's not necessarily a spokesman for a generation, but all that's in the music... the passion (and the fact that) he doesn't necessarily know what he wants, but he's pissed. It's all these things working at different levels at once. I don't exactly know what 'Teen Spirit' means, but you know it means *something* , and it's intense as hell."

BUTCH VIG, PRODUCER OF *NEVERMIND*, 1992

"Free us from Nancy Spungen fixated heroin a-holes who cling to our greatest rock groups and suck out their brains."

JULIAN COPE ON COURTNEY LOVE

"I went to an all-ages show in Tacoma at the Community world theatre in 1987. One band had a singer with long hair and a drummer with short hair and a moustache. They played Creedence Clearwater Revival songs. I didn't think much of it. Months later, I went to see Nirvana at the Vogue in Seattle. I thought I recognised the long-haired singer on stage. 'Oh,' it occurred to me, 'these are the guys that do the Creedence covers'." **HOLE'S PATTY SCHEMEL**

WHAT THEY SAID ABOUT KURT & **COURTNEY**

"We were happy to have creative and interesting people here, they (Kurt and Courtney) were exemplary neighbours."
THE COBAIN'S NEIGHBOURS, ON HEARING OF KURT'S SUICIDE

"I don't think any of us would be in this room tonight if it weren't for Kurt Cobain." PEARL JAM'S EDDIE VEDDER TO HIS AUDIENCE THE NIGHT AFTER KURT'S BODY WAS FOUND

"Kurt could just be very outgoing and funny and charming, and a half hour later he would just go sit in the corner and be totally moody and uncommunicative. And, I would ask Krist. 'Is he OK?' and Krist would say, 'He's alright... sometimes he's just quiet'. And then he'd be fine again." BUTCH VIG

EDDIE VEDDER

"Our bands were playing the Reading Festival in 1991, just before *Nevermind* went ballistic. Toward the end of an absolutely raging set, Kurt leapt over the monitors and into the photo pit where Dave Markey just happened to be shooting our tour film, *The Year Punk Broke*. Hundreds of arms reached out to grab him. Kurt still playing, made his way over to Markey, stuck his mouth to the camera mike, and said, 'This is a blues scale in E', poking fun at himself and every guitar hero ever."
SONIC YOUTH'S LEE RENALDO ON HIS FONDEST MEMORY OF KURT

"I think about Kurt everyday and I miss him, and I realise that I miss him. But at the same time things keep going and I've got to make sure that things keep moving

for me. I don't know if this band (Foo Fighters) makes anyone else feel better, I just know I have to do it for myself. I have to feel like I'm moving forward.' **99** DAVE GROHL, 1995

66 Courtney is such a miserable person. When I met her, when I was trying to sign her, she spent the whole time slagging off her husband. She was saying, 'Oh, Hole are so much better than Nirvana' and just going off on a tangent. She just loves to hear herself talk. She doesn't even mean half the things she says, she's just incredibly competitive with people and anybody who's successful she's going to slag off. That's all there is to it. I think she's really talented but she's got to find something to hang on to and she's got to find happiness. If she doesn't, then I don't know what will become of her. That goes for everybody. **99** MADONNA, 1995

66 Do I have sympathy for Courtney? … I suppose I feel bad that she's lost somebody that she obviously loved, but it's not like it was a great surprise to anybody. When you take that many drugs it's only a matter of time, you now what I mean? And let's face it, she's where she is because she put herself there. She's not a victim. 99 MADONNA, 1995

MICHAEL STIPE

66 In the last few weeks I was talking to Kurt a lot… We had a musical project in the works, but nothing was recorded. He loved Courtney and Frances Bean, and he loved Krist and Dave and Nirvana. He really loved those guys. His death is a profound loss, and I really don't think I can say anything else right now. **99**

MICHAEL STIPE, R.E.M., 1994

WHAT THEY SAID ABOUT KURT & COURTNEY

"I was simply blown away when I found out that Kurt Cobain liked my work, and I always wanted to talk to him about his reasons for covering 'Man Who Sold The World'. It was a straightforward rendition and sounded somehow very honest. It would have been nice to work with him, but just talking would have been real cool." DAVID BOWIE

"Everyone was so fascinated by Nirvana because they sold so many records, why can't they be fascinated by them because that guy writes really good lyrics and they rock.**"**

CHRIS ROBINSON, THE BLACK CROWS

"Remember Kurt for what he was: caring, generous and sweet. Let's keep the music with us. We'll always have it forever."

KRIST NOVOSELIC

"We were doing a show at the Mississippi Nights club in St. Louis on the *Nevermind* tour, and the whole day there had been this running joke in the Nirvana camp about how Guns N' Roses had just had that big riot there. Kurt mentioned that he'd like to start a riot, too, but I don't think anyone took him seriously. Nirvana needed to use our gear that night because the previous evening they had just trashed *everything*. It was only 20 minutes into their set and Dave runs in and says that Kurt just invited the entire club onstage because there was so many kids stage-diving. We realised our gear was up-there, so we all went running on stage to save our equipment. We found Krist and Kurt sitting on the edge of the stage, totally bewildered, with 500 kids swarming all around them. The whole place was going crazy, the owners were calling the cops. The police showed up and Krist gave this long speech how everybody needed to get along and he talked everybody back in to their seats and the cops agreed not to arrest anybody. Nirvana started playing again and they kept the club open late so they could finish their set. Even the cops stayed and watched the show, What started out as total mayhem ended in peaceful resolution. That's how badly people wanted to hear Nirvana.**"**

BLACKIE ONASSIS, URGE OVERKILL

"On the one hand, she is the most vulnerable, innocent, sensitive, generous girl. On the other hand, I'm telling you, she could be tougher than nails on Christ's cross. And then she has the courage not to hide any of the levels or shades of her personality, and calls for it and puts it all there on the screen. That's something which I'm fascinated to watch." MILOS FORMAN, 1997

"Courtney will ring me even to discuss what outfit she will wear onstage that night. I love working with her. She is a huge celebrity, one of the top two or three familiar images in America. We have that from a survey in *Brand Week* magazine which shows she has an 11 per cent recognition factor, which is third highest of any woman." **MANAGER PETER MENSCH, 1997**

"I liked her a lot. She was open and honest. One time I knocked on her door, she says, Yeah! and there she is doing her make-up, wearing nothing but a pair of tights. She says, 'Come in for fuck's sake, haven't you see a pair of tits before?' I perch on a chair, staring at the ceiling and she says, 'What's the matter with you? They're good tits, aren't they?'" ANONYMOUS TOUR PROMOTER, 1999

"She was always looking at magazines and if she read that Madonna had gone to a particular hair stylist then she wanted to be booked in there immediately." **MAKE UP ARTIST, LOS ANGELES, 1999**

"Courtney's definitely an extraordinary person. I found her quite easy to work with. Her mind moves quickly, and so does mine." JORDAN ZADOROXNY (BLINKER), 1997

66When I interviewed her in 1994 she was amazingly frank. She actually said 'You need to know everything.' Halfway through, she went to the toilet still talking, left the door open, sat there having a piss with a fag in her mouth and incredibly expensive knickers round her ankles, squeezed a spot on her chin, and did an impersonation of Julian Cope. Then when she was leaving she said, 'Be honest about me or I will hit you, my husband will shoot you and we will both sue.'99 **CAITLIN MORAN**, *THE TIMES*, 2001

66**Of course she's an appalling monster, but she's also very intelligent and funny and a huge vindication for young women.**99

CAITLIN MORAN, *THE TIMES*, 2001

66If one definition of great music is that it has to be extreme, up to '95 Courtney was one of the three most compelling performers I've ever seen. She was only interested in expressing herself. She was never afraid to make a fool of herself onstage. She lived and died there.99 **JOURNALIST EVERETT TRUE**, 2001

66**I watched her from one of the first UK gigs, at the Underworld (1991). I don't think she's about being a brilliant musician. She's one of the most charismatic people I've ever met. Until you meet her you wouldn't believe it because we can stagger around and be a bit of an embarrassment.**99 AMY RAPHAEL, *ESQUIRE*, 2001

WHAT THEY SAID ABOUT KURT & **COURTNEY**

" Love is a complete alien to Nirvana's music and success who is trying to prohibit the remaining members of Nirvana from any commercial exploitation of the music they created. "

GROHL AND NOVOSELIC'S RESPONSE TO THE COURT DEPOSITION, 2001

DAVE GROHL

" I think she's doing all of this so people will continue to care about her. It's much easier than putting a new album out. Pop a few pills, talk some shit, don't sit down on a plane, get arrested, get some press. Makes sense to me. "

BUDDYHEAD'S TRAVIS KELLER, 2003

" Courtney is a true iconoclast and star. She truly rocked the club. The best bit for me was when she stuck on (Adam & The Ants) 'Antmusic' and ran into the sweaty throng. She's a true rock'n'roll star. " **ALAN MCGEE AT LONDON'S METRO CLUB, 2003**

" She's incredibly articulate, well read and very well-educated. I'm the exact opposite. I'm inarticulate, not well-educated, but there is something that we share that's rare. Really rare. And that is... an incredible ambition and drive. And growing up in the Eighties, those were the things we'd think of as bad words. The drive and the ambition is coming from somewhere else. " MICHAEL STIPE, 1999

" I like Courtney, but she's fuckin' bonkers. "

MUDHONEY'S MARK ARM, 1995

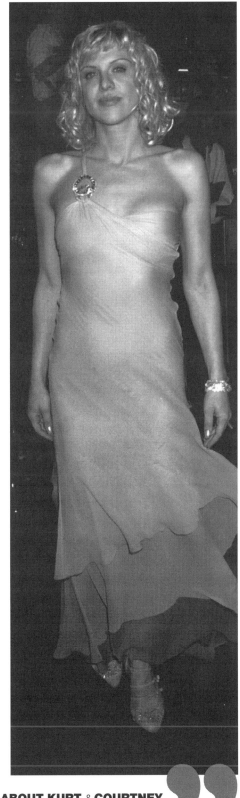

"She tore Kurt apart. Nothing Kurt Cobain could do could make Courtney happy. If he did kill himself, I know why!"

LOVE'S FATHER HANK HARRISON, 1996

"I don't in any way have anything personally against Courtney, I just think a lot of the things she does are quite misguided.**"**

KURT & COURTNEY DOCUMENTARY-MAKER NICK BROOMFIELD, 1998

"It's a weird thing now – you just yearn for Kurt. It's only when you hear the new Pearl Jam record that you realise how much you fucking miss him. There's this howling noise that screams from the depths of your soul – why on earth did you have to leave us? I don't think he'd got any concept of how much people here genuinely loved him."

RADIO 1 DJ MARY ANN HOBBS, 1998

"There have been other pieces and films made about Courtney that have simply never come out because of pressure from her PR people. It nearly happened to this one. So there's a lot of internal censorship, for example, on the part of companies like MTV who depend on being able to show Nirvana videos.**"**

KURT & COURTNEY DOCUMENTARY-MAKER NICK BROOMFIELD, 1998

WHAT THEY SAID ABOUT KURT & COURTNEY

The Last Word

"The American public really does want me to die. I'm not going to die.**"** **COURTNEY, 1995**